STERLING BIOGRAPHIES

FRANKLIN DELANO ROOSEVELT

A National Hero

Sudipta Bardhan-Quallen

Sterling Publishing Co., Inc.
New York

Library of Congress Cataloging-in-Publication Data

Bardhan-Quallen, Sudipta.
  Franklin D. Roosevelt : our national hero / Sudipta Bardhan-Quallen.
      p. cm. — (Sterling biographies)
  Includes bibliographical references and index.
  ISBN-13: 978-1-4027-3545-5
  ISBN-10: 1-4027-3545-6
  1. Roosevelt, Franklin D. (Franklin Delano), 1882-1945—Juvenile literature.
  2. Presidents—United States—Biography—Juvenile literature. I. Title.

E807.B27 2007
973.917092—dc22
[B]
                                                    2006027187

10 9 7 6 5 4 3 2 1

Published by Sterling Publishing Co., Inc.
387 Park Avenue South, New York, NY 10016
© 2007 by Sudipta Bardhan-Quallen
Distributed in Canada by Sterling Publishing
C/o Canadian Manda Group, 165 Dufferin Street
Toronto, Ontaa M6K 3H6
Distributed in the United Kingdom by GMC Distribution Services
Castle Place, 166 High Street, Lewes, East Sussex, England BN7 1XU
Distributed in Australia by Capricorn Link (Australia) Pty. Ltd.
P.O. Box 704, Windsor, NSW 2756, Australia

Sterling ISBN-13: 978-1-4027-3545-5 (paperback)
      ISBN-10: 1-4027-3545-6

Sterling ISBN-13: 978-1-4027-4747-2 (hardcover)
      ISBN-10: 1-4027-4747-0

Paged by Dopodomani
Image research by Susan Schader

For information about custom editions, special sales, and premium
and corporate purchases, please contact Sterling Special Sales
Department at 800-805-5489 or specialsales@sterlingpub.com.

Contents

Events in the Life of Franklin Delano Roosevelt

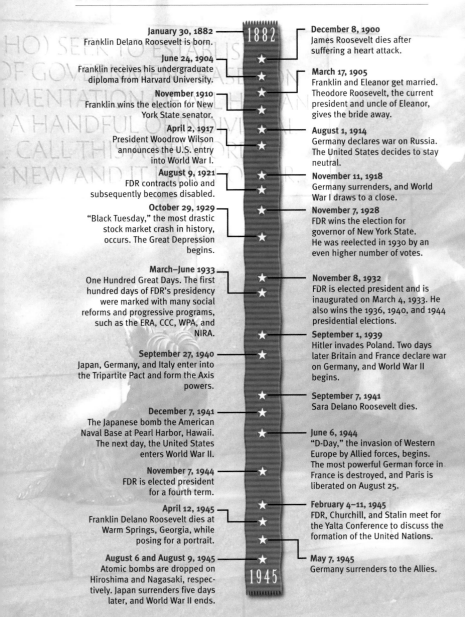

January 30, 1882
Franklin Delano Roosevelt is born.

June 24, 1904
Franklin receives his undergraduate diploma from Harvard University.

November 1910
Franklin wins the election for New York State senator.

April 2, 1917
President Woodrow Wilson announces the U.S. entry into World War I.

August 9, 1921
FDR contracts polio and subsequently becomes disabled.

October 29, 1929
"Black Tuesday," the most drastic stock market crash in history, occurs. The Great Depression begins.

March–June 1933
One Hundred Great Days. The first hundred days of FDR's presidency were marked with many social reforms and progressive programs, such as the ERA, CCC, WPA, and NIRA.

September 27, 1940
Japan, Germany, and Italy enter into the Tripartite Pact and form the Axis powers.

December 7, 1941
The Japanese bomb the American Naval Base at Pearl Harbor, Hawaii. The next day, the United States enters World War II.

November 7, 1944
FDR is elected president for a fourth term.

April 12, 1945
Franklin Delano Roosevelt dies at Warm Springs, Georgia, while posing for a portrait.

August 6 and August 9, 1945
Atomic bombs are dropped on Hiroshima and Nagasaki, respectively. Japan surrenders five days later, and World War II ends.

1882

December 8, 1900
James Roosevelt dies after suffering a heart attack.

March 17, 1905
Franklin and Eleanor get married. Theodore Roosevelt, the current president and uncle of Eleanor, gives the bride away.

August 1, 1914
Germany declares war on Russia. The United States decides to stay neutral.

November 11, 1918
Germany surrenders, and World War I draws to a close.

November 7, 1928
FDR wins the election for governor of New York State. He was reelected in 1930 by an even higher number of votes.

November 8, 1932
FDR is elected president and is inaugurated on March 4, 1933. He also wins the 1936, 1940, and 1944 presidential elections.

September 1, 1939
Hitler invades Poland. Two days later Britain and France declare war on Germany, and World War II begins.

September 7, 1941
Sara Delano Roosevelt dies.

June 6, 1944
"D-Day," the invasion of Western Europe by Allied forces, begins. The most powerful German force in France is destroyed, and Paris is liberated on August 25.

February 4–11, 1945
FDR, Churchill, and Stalin meet for the Yalta Conference to discuss the formation of the United Nations.

May 7, 1945
Germany surrenders to the Allies.

1945

Vision and Guidance

There is no time for fear, for reaction or timidity. . . . I pledge myself to a new deal for the American people.

The summer before Franklin Delano Roosevelt was **inaugurated** into his first term as president of the United States in 1933, a reporter asked the famous British economist John Maynard Keynes to comment on the state of the world's economy. A historic economic slump called the **Great Depression** was raging in the United States, and things looked bleak all over the world. The reporter asked Keynes if the world had ever seen anything like the Great Depression before. Keynes replied, "Yes, it was called the Dark Ages, and it lasted four hundred years."

Roosevelt fully understood the seriousness of the situation in the country as he assumed office—and in case he did not, there were plenty of people to remind him. Outgoing president Herbert Hoover was one of them. As late as one a.m. on

As Americans' spending power fell during the Great Depression, many businesses failed, putting even more people out of work. Vacant storefronts like the ones seen here were a common sight.

the morning of the inauguration, Hoover was arguing with Franklin about the best course of action for the future. A few days after Roosevelt took office, a visitor told him, "Mr. President, if your program succeeds, you'll be the greatest president in American history. If it fails, you will be the worst one." Roosevelt replied, "If it fails, I'll be the last one."

During World War II, FDR (center, seated) met with Joseph Stalin (left, seated) and Winston Churchill (right, seated) in Teheran in 1943.

Luckily for Americans, Franklin Delano Roosevelt (often referred to as FDR) led the country through the crisis of the Great Depression—in thirteen years, not four hundred. He proved his expertise again as he steered the United States through another crisis, World War II. Through his vision and guidance, FDR's presidency left the nation stronger and facing a bright future.

CHAPTER 1

A Privileged Youth

The highest idea I could hold up before our boy—
to grow to be . . . an upstanding American.

    –Sara Delano Roosevelt

By the time the baby was born, even the nurse thought there was no way he would survive. He was quiet, blue, and alarmingly still. His mother, Sara Delano Roosevelt, had been in labor for more than twenty-four hours and had lost consciousness. However, the physician at Sara's bedside, Dr. Edward H. Parker, decided to blow air into the baby's lungs to try to get him to breathe—and it worked. The ten-pound Roosevelt baby took some shuddering breaths and began to wail. It was January 30, 1882.

It took almost two months to give the new "baby Roosevelt" a name—his father, James Roosevelt, wanted to name him Isaac after his own father, but Sara preferred to name the boy Warren after her father. As it turned out, he would not be named Isaac or Warren. When the christening was held

Franklin's difficult birth led to a particularly close bond with his mother, Sara.

on March 20, the baby's official name became Franklin Delano Roosevelt after his great-uncle Franklin Hughes Delano.

A Well-Loved Child

Franklin was greatly loved by his parents. Franklin's father, James, was a slender man of medium height, with hazel eyes and muttonchop whiskers. He was fifty-four years old when Franklin was born, but he was determined not to let his age interfere with his parenting. James was fond of the outdoors, and he taught Franklin to love nature. From the time Franklin was four years old, father and son went sledding, skating, and horseback riding together. James also taught his son how to sail an iceboat and a yacht and to shoot.

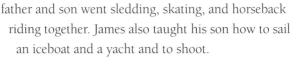

This 1883 photograph shows a 16-month old Franklin poised on his father James's shoulder.

Franklin was close to both his parents, but his bond with his mother, Sara, was especially strong. Sara could not have any more children after Franklin, so she lavished all of her maternal love on her only son. She supervised every part of Franklin's early life: "Up at seven. Breakfast at eight. Lessons

Eleven-year-old Franklin, dressed in riding togs, posed in a New York studio. Perhaps he was looking forward to a ride on his pony, Debbie.

from nine to noon. An hour in which to play, then lunch and more lessons until four. Two more hours to play games, of which his mother approved. Then, supper at six and bed by eight. Day after day."

Franklin spent almost all of his early years with his parents. Sara was reluctant to leave Franklin's side, so he was almost always in the company of adults instead of other children. The Roosevelt family home, Springwood, was in Hyde Park, New York, but whenever Franklin's parents traveled, which was often, he went with them. By the time he was three years old, Franklin's regular travels included his mother's family home in Fairhaven, Massachusetts; Roosevelt's summerhouse on Campobello, an island in New Brunswick, Canada, near the coast of Maine; and even Great Britain. They traveled by luxury ocean liner or in James Roosevelt's private railroad car, the Monon.

In the winter of 1887, when Franklin was five years old, his father took him to the White House for the first time. James's friend, Grover Cleveland, was the president, and the Roosevelts had been invited to visit. Cleveland, terribly burdened by the responsibilities of the presidency, made a wish on Franklin's behalf when they said good-bye: "My little man, I am making a strange wish for you. It is that you may never be president of the United States."

President Grover Cleveland invited the Roosevelts to visit the White House in 1887; it was Franklin's first visit to the national landmark which would later become his home.

Roosevelts in the New World

Around 1650, Claes Martenszen van Rosenvelt immigrated to America from the Netherlands. He settled in New York. Claes had a son named Nicholas and three grandsons. One grandson, Johannes, was the ancestor of Theodore Roosevelt. Another grandson, Jacobus, was the ancestor of Isaac Roosevelt, known in the family as "the patriot." Isaac joined the American revolutionary cause and voted for independence as a delegate to the Provincial Congress of 1776. Isaac's great-great-grandson would also be hailed as a patriot—his name was Franklin Delano Roosevelt.

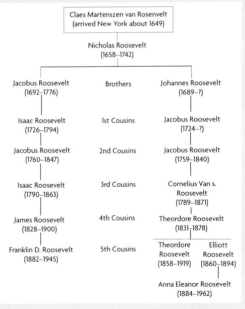

The Roosevelt family tree, showing both the Hyde Park (Franklin's) and Oyster Bay (Eleanor's) branches of the family.

Both James Roosevelt and Sara Delano came from wealthy families. By the age of seven, Franklin fully understood that James and Sara were important people, and that made him important as well. However, his parents wanted to make sure that Franklin would not take the privileges of wealth for granted, and that Franklin grow up knowing he was expected to act like a gentleman at all times. As Sara said, "The highest idea I could hold up before our boy—to grow to be like his father, straight and honorable, just and kind, an upstanding American."

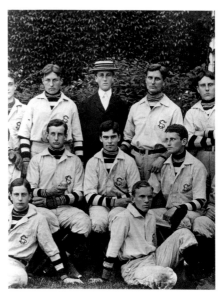

Franklin (top row, wearing a hat) played for Groton's second-string baseball team, known as the Bum Base Ball Boys.

Groton Life

To help Franklin reach Sara's goals for him, he was enrolled in Groton in 1896, an exclusive private school in Massachusetts. Because Sara preferred to have her son at home, Franklin was educated by tutors during his early years. He didn't start at Groton until he was fourteen years old, instead of at twelve like the other boys.

After leaving Franklin behind at Groton, Sara wrote: "It is hard to leave our darling boy. James and I feel this parting very much." This was the first time Franklin was out on his own,

The first and second football squads at the Groton School. Franklin (seated in the front row, second from the left) had to struggle to earn a spot on the second squad.

without his parents' watchful eyes. It was also the first time that Franklin was not completely surrounded by luxury.

Though all of the students at Groton came from wealthy families, the school itself lacked many of the comforts that boys like Franklin were used to. A bell woke all the students up at 6:45 a.m. Immediately, the boys rushed to large common bathrooms, which had only cold running water. Every boy took an icy shower in the morning, but not in individual stalls. Instead, a group of loud, pushing, naked boys waited in line to take a turn under the showerheads.

Franklin was a smart young man, so schoolwork came easily to him. Fitting in with other boys his age, however, was much harder. It didn't help that Franklin joined his class two years after

Getting Along with the Fellows

Franklin always told his parents that he was "getting along finely both mentally and physically" at Groton, but this was not always true. One day, after Franklin arrived at school, a group of older boys trapped him in a hallway, jabbed at his ankles with their hockey sticks, and yelled, "dance!" Franklin, however, refused to be a victim—he danced and twirled as if he were part of the fun, rather than the one who was being teased. He seemed so fearless that the older boys soon lost interest and let him go.

everyone else had begun school or that Franklin had so little experience with other people his own age. Furthermore, at Groton, athletic ability was highly prized, but Franklin did not play sports such as football or baseball well. In fact, when he played baseball, he was placed on "a new team called the BBBB or Bum Base Ball Boys" —made up entirely of the worst players in the school.

Also, all the time spent in Europe had given Franklin a distinctive accent and overly refined manners. He used to bow to the headmaster's wife every evening until he was told not to do so. The other students were not brought up with as much of a European influence. They did not realize that Franklin was not being snobby; he was just imitating what he had seen others do during his childhood in Europe. In a letter to his parents on May 24, 1899, Franklin wrote his thanks for receiving British magazines: "Many thanks for *Punch* and *Spectator*. They were most welcome to me, [though] hardly appreciated by others, as they are 'so English you know.'" Later, Franklin confessed that he was "always a little the outsider" at Groton.

Despite his social difficulties, a lot of positive things came out of Franklin's years at Groton. Franklin had the opportunity to hear many influential people speak, such as his distant cousin, Theodore Roosevelt, who was a frequent visitor. Theodore's speeches helped to influence Franklin's view on public service.

Cousin Theodore

By the time Theodore was a guest speaker at Franklin's school, he had already had a distinguished career: Between 1882 and 1884, Theodore had been elected as a Republican member of the New York State Assembly, the elected body that makes laws for New York State. He then moved on to appointments as the police commissioner of New York City in 1895 and as the assistant secretary of the U.S. Navy in 1897. In 1898, he resigned from his post in the navy in order to help organize a volunteer regiment, the Rough Riders, during the Spanish-American War. That same year Theodore was elected governor of New York. Later, in 1897, Theodore was elected as vice president, and in 1901, became president of the United States when President William McKinley was assassinated.

Franklin so admired his cousin Theodore that he wore a similar style of eyeglasses.

Franklin's genuine admiration for his cousin made him eager to follow in Theodore's footsteps. This admiration showed itself in other ways as well. When Franklin was told in 1899 that he needed to wear glasses, he ordered a gold-rimmed pair in the pince-nez style—exactly like Theodore's.

CHAPTER 2

Making His Own Way

"The strife is o'er, the battle won!"
What a joyful yet sad day this has been.

Franklin graduated from Groton in the spring of 1900. On his last day there, he wrote to his parents: " 'The strife is o'er, the battle won!' What a joyful yet sad day this has been." A big chapter of his life had reached its conclusion.

By that fall, Franklin was a student at Harvard University in Cambridge, Massachusetts. Overall, just as at Groton, Franklin was not altogether accepted by the other students. Not letting that deter him, he joined the Republican Club of Harvard in order to support Theodore's vice-presidential run with William McKinley.

Franklin (top row, second from the left) with his classmates from Harvard in 1904, at Nantasket Beach, Massachusetts.

During his Harvard years, Franklin became very interested in politics. He decided to run for office at Harvard. In 1903, he was one of six candidates who ran for the office of class marshal—but it was not a fair election. Because Harvard had many clubs, votes could be secured from the club memberships for specific candidates. The three men who received the most votes would win, so Franklin thought the election had become a popularity contest instead of a fair competition. Just as at Groton, Franklin was an outsider at Harvard, and he had no chance of winning. He was not popular enough with the clubs to earn the votes he needed. He wrote on December 16, 1903: "The election is going on all day—I don't stand the least show—in fact will get less votes than any of the others for marshal." Still, Franklin did not give up. Right after the class marshal elections, he campaigned for another office: chairman of the 1904 class committee. When the votes were tallied, Franklin had received 168, or 66 percent, of the 253 votes cast. It was the first election in his life that Franklin won.

During his Harvard years, Franklin became very interested in politics. He decided to run for office at Harvard.

In 1904, Franklin became editor in chief of the student newspaper, *The Harvard Crimson.* He was proud of this appointment and counted it as one of the greatest achievements of his Harvard career.

Personal Changes

A tragedy struck the Roosevelt family during Franklin's first term at Harvard. On December 8, 1900, his father, James Roosevelt, died after suffering a heart attack. The Roosevelts grieved deeply for James, and the bond between Sara and Franklin grew even stronger after James's death as Sara relied much more heavily on her son. Franklin, however, was nearing a point in his life at which he wanted to strike out on his own. He was even more sure of this after he became reacquainted with his distant cousin, Anna Eleanor Roosevelt.

Eleanor was the daughter of Anna Hall and Elliott Roosevelt, members of the Oyster Bay, New York, branch of the wealthy and influential Roosevelt clan. When Eleanor was fourteen years old, Franklin had danced with her at a Christmas party. He enjoyed her company and said that she had "a very good mind." Years later, on November 17, 1902, the pair met again; this time Franklin saw Eleanor with friends at the New York Horse Show at Madison Square Garden. After that, the two met often for lunch or tea or at parties.

A Perfect Pair

In many ways, Eleanor opened Franklin's eyes to a world that his mother had sheltered him from for years. Though Eleanor was from a wealthy family, and the niece of the current president, she felt strongly about helping those less fortunate than herself. Eleanor worked in New York City's Rivington Street Settlement House helping young immigrants adjust to life in America.

Fifteen-year-old Eleanor at Allenwood School, run by Madame Souvestre, of whom Eleanor would later say, "She shocked me into thinking."

Eleanor also saw overcrowded tenements and factories exploiting women and children workers, and she put her efforts into exposing these harsh working conditions. Eleanor introduced Franklin to this world when he would meet her after work at the Settlement House. On one occasion, the young couple helped a sick girl get back to her home in a tenement. Franklin was horrified by the living conditions there. He "could not believe human beings lived that way."

Eleanor's social work among poor Manhattan families, such as the one shown here, gave future president Franklin insight into how the underprivileged lived.

But the Roosevelts' courtship was not just about exposing social injustices. Franklin and Eleanor went to the White House on New Year's Day, and Franklin noted in his diary, "sat near Eleanor. Very interesting day." Eleanor was also a guest at Franklin's birthday celebration in 1903 and came to Springwood for a four-day visit that June. Each encounter, however, was hardly private—there was always a chaperone present. Even their personal letters followed strict rules. As Eleanor explained, "You knew a man very well before you wrote or received a letter from him . . . and to have signed one in any other way than 'very sincerely yours' would have been not only a breach of good manners but an admission of feeling which was entirely inadmissible."

By 1903, Franklin had decided to marry Eleanor. They became engaged on November 21. Years later, Eleanor confessed

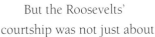

that, before she accepted his proposal, Franklin told her that he would make something of himself with her help.

While Franklin's sentiment was touching, it was also a true statement. After all, at the time of their engagement, Eleanor was the more distinguished Roosevelt—she was the direct relative of the president, and her branch of the Roosevelt clan could come and go freely at places such as the White House, where their favorite son, Theodore, was chief executive. For Franklin, who had always felt like an outsider, marriage to Eleanor gave him an opportunity to be accepted and to feel like he fit in with an important group of people.

Ambition was not Franklin's only reason to marry Eleanor. By all accounts, he was very much in love with her. In his private diaries, he called Eleanor "an angel" and "my darling." Even though his mother was not enthusiastic about Franklin and Eleanor's plans to marry—she even made the couple keep the engagement secret for a whole year—Franklin did not give up on his fiancée. He wrote a number of letters to his mother to convince her to accept Eleanor. On December 4, 1903, he wrote: "I am the happiest man just now in the world: likewise, the luckiest— And for you, dear Mummy, you know that nothing can ever change what we have & always will be to each

Eleanor on her wedding day in 1905. She was "given away" by her uncle, President Theodore Roosevelt.

other—only now you have two children to love & to love you." All the while, Franklin waited impatiently to be able to tell the world about his upcoming wedding.

Franklin with Eleanor in Campobello in 1904, during their secret engagement.

A New Partnership

While he waited, Franklin completed his coursework at Harvard. On June 24, 1904, he received his diploma. Sara and Eleanor were both in the audience to celebrate with Franklin. He then moved on to start law school at Columbia University in New York.

But when it finally came time to tell the world—starting with the Delano side of his family—about the engagement, to his great disappointment, Franklin fell ill. Instead of being able to tell them the happy news himself over the Thanksgiving table at Fairhaven, Franklin was forced to stay home and recuperate while a letter was read to his family. Nevertheless, the Delanos were extremely pleased. After the official engagement announcement was published in newspapers, a blizzard of letters to congratulate the couple came in, including one from Theodore in the White House. Theodore wrote to Franklin: "I am as fond of Eleanor as if she were my daughter; and I like you, and trust you, and believe in you." Theodore even agreed to give the bride away at the wedding, set for March 17, 1905.

From that point on, Theodore was extremely generous to Franklin and Eleanor. His letters to Franklin were signed, "your

Overshadowed at the Ceremony

The wedding of Franklin and Eleanor was held on East Seventy-sixth Street in New York City, at the home of Eleanor's cousins, with whom she lived. The bride was given away by her uncle, the president, who delayed the ceremony by arriving late.

Theodore Roosevelt stole the show a bit. When asked who gave Eleanor in marriage, rather than simply placing the bride's hand in the groom's, Theodore answered loudly, "*I do!*" Later, he led the new couple into the dining room, with most of the guests trailing after the president rather than the new Mr. and Mrs. Franklin Delano Roosevelt. Even the cake cutting was of no interest to most people until Theodore went to

Teddy Roosevelt at Franklin and Eleanor's wedding.

witness it. Still, Franklin and Eleanor were glad to have Theodore there, and he blessed the couple again, saying to Franklin, "There's nothing like keeping the name in the family."

affectionate uncle," a clear indication that Theodore felt true warmth for Franklin. When Theodore's second inauguration was held on March 4, 1905, the president invited Franklin and Eleanor to the festivities. He seated the couple in a place of honor behind his own family. At the inauguration, Franklin heard Theodore promise every American "a square deal"—a sentiment that would influence Franklin later in his own political life.

At the inauguration, Franklin heard Theodore promise every American "a square deal"—a sentiment that would influence Franklin later in his own political life.

For the next two years, Franklin continued to attend Columbia Law School, but he never graduated. He did, however, pass the bar exam in the spring of 1907, and he began to practice law. He landed a position with a Wall Street firm called Carter, Ledyard and Milburn, but his heart was not in being a lawyer. Within a few years, Franklin's interests turned to something that he considered more worthy of his ancestry.

Marital Memories

Later in life, after becoming president, when FDR was introduced to a newly engaged couple, he made it a point to congratulate them both equally. His secretary, Grace Tully, once asked him why he did that. She remembered: "He quickly explained that he [had] felt the need for it at the time of his engagement. He said that when his engagement was announced, all the congratulations were showered on him for securing Eleanor as a wife. He felt that some people at least should have congratulated her for securing him as a husband."

CHAPTER 3

Life in Politics Begins

*I get my fingers into everything
and there's no law against it.*

After Franklin and Eleanor's wedding, the couple moved into a house in New York City that Franklin's mother had rented and furnished for them while they were on their honeymoon. Early in their marriage, Sara dominated Franklin and Eleanor's lives. Sara was unwilling to distance herself from her son, so she built a double townhouse at 49 East 65th Street. She gave half to Franklin and Eleanor and kept the other half for herself. On each floor of the house, there were sliding doors connecting both halves. Eleanor wrote that there was never any privacy, day or night—Sara was always part of the scene.

Sara's influence was far-reaching because she controlled the money in her son's household. So whatever she said, went. When Sara wanted Eleanor to give up her social work, Eleanor did.

This townhouse at 125 East 36th Street was the young Roosevelts' first home together.

Within the first four years of their marriage, Franklin and Eleanor had three children: Anna Eleanor Roosevelt, born in 1906; James Roosevelt, born in 1907; and Franklin Delano Roosevelt, Junior, born in 1909. Though Franklin Junior did not survive infancy, the Roosevelts continued to build their family. Elliott was born in 1910, followed by another Franklin Junior in 1914. Finally, the Roosevelt's last child, John Aspinwall Roosevelt, was born in 1916.

The Roosevelts as Parents

The Roosevelt children essentially had three parents in their home—Franklin, Eleanor, and Sara. Each of the adult Roosevelts handled parenthood very differently. The children adored Franklin, as he was the one to come home from work and play with them. He was rarely involved in disciplining the children or in other aspects of raising them.

Sara was as much a presence in her grandchildren's lives as she was in her son's life. As Eleanor recalled, "Franklin's children were more my mother-in-law's children . . . than they were mine." The children went to Sara to be spoiled. She gave them more love and warmth than they could get from their mother. Said Eleanor's niece, "They [the Roosevelt children] learned early that if their mother wouldn't give them something, all they had to do was to go see Granny. And they could charm Granny out of anything they wanted."

Franklin shared a special bond with Anna, the couple's first child and only daughter.

Family Tragedy

Both Franklin and Eleanor wanted a large family, and as with most things in their lives, they seemed to get what they wanted. This is not to say, however, that the privileged Roosevelts did not experience heartbreak as well. Though the first Franklin Junior had been born a healthy eleven-pound baby, when he was seven months old, he developed a heart condition. He died on November 2, 1909.

Eleanor was crushed by her son's death. She had to be forced to leave the grave site, and later said, "How cruel it seemed to leave him out there alone in the cold." Franklin's response to his son's death was to join the New York Milk Committee, an organization that tried to fight infant mortality.

Eleanor loved her children but was largely overwhelmed by motherhood. She really did not know what to do, and so she often did quite unusual things to her children. Eleanor tied their arms to their sides so that the children would not suck their thumbs. Once, to let one of the babies get fresh air, she hung the cradle outside a window like a window box—a fairly scary proposition—until a neighbor threatened to call the authorities. These failed attempts at proper motherhood made Eleanor feel even less able to cope with her children.

Furthermore, since Franklin and Sara indulged the children, Eleanor was left to be the disciplinarian. She said, "It did not come naturally to me to understand little children or to enjoy them. Playing with children was difficult for me because play had not been an important part of my own childhood." The parenting differences among Eleanor, Franklin, and Sara were noticed by most people; and Sara even commented to the children that their mother was only a mother in that she gave them life.

Public Office

While the Roosevelt family grew, FDR discovered a new path for himself in politics. In 1910, the Dutchess County district attorney, Judge John E. Mack, came to drop off some papers to be signed at FDR's law offices. By the end of the visit, Mack had encouraged FDR to run for a seat in the New York State Senate as a Democrat.

Eleanor with James, left; Elliot, center; and Anna, right. Eleanor's unhappy childhood left her unprepared for motherhood; she looked to her mother-in-law, Sara, for advice on "almost every subject."

Franklin D. Roosevelt

For State Senator

A poster for Franklin's first campaign, for New York State senator. It would be the first of many victories for FDR.

When he formally accepted the nomination to run, from the Dutchess County Democrats, FDR said, "I thank you for giving me an opportunity to advance the cause of good government under the banner of the Democratic Party this year. I accept this nomination with absolute independence. I am pledged to no man; I am influenced by no special interests, and so I shall remain."

The district FDR was trying to represent was overwhelmingly Republican, so it was assumed that a Democrat would have a hard time winning the election. This campaign gave FDR the opportunity to learn many of the techniques that would make him a very successful politician. He learned to address large crowds of undecided voters as "My friends" to sway their minds toward him. He also had a knack for turning misfortune into political gain. On one occasion, FDR's campaign car ran over a dog. There were no witnesses, so FDR could have chosen to flee the scene and avoid a potentially embarrassing situation. Instead, he sought out the dog's owner and insisted on paying the man reparations of five dollars. By doing this, FDR turned the whole episode into a vote-winner.

FDR's campaign took a lot of energy, and the candidate spent many long hours on the road meeting voters every day. The efforts paid off. He impressed voters with his exuberance, warmth, and intelligence. On Election Day, when the votes were counted, Franklin Roosevelt received 15,708 votes—1,140 more than his Republican opponent. Finally, at the age of twenty-eight, FDR had started the career that would make history.

A Free Spirit

From FDR's first term as a state senator, he was determined to be his own man. He decided that he would not give in to the **party bosses** who, in FDR's opinion, were dishonest and only worked for their own gain. His first opportunity to stand up to

FDR's efforts against his fellow state senator, Republican Chauncey Depew, assured that a Democrat would represent New York in Washington, D.C.

these bosses came early on. In those days, two U.S. senators were chosen for each state by state legislatures. FDR's 86 Republican colleagues supported the incumbent U.S. senator, Chauncey Depew. The 114 Democrats in the state senate, however, had split support between William F. Sheehan, the choice of the party bosses, and Edward Shepard, a respected lawyer. FDR supported Shepard, whom he believed would stand against corruption and would work to **reform** the political system.

Louis Howe

Louis McHenry Howe was a political journalist who first met Roosevelt in 1911 while reporting on FDR's battle against the party bosses. He eventually became FDR's right-hand man. Howe became his chief of staff even before FDR's presidential administration and evolved to be his most trusted advisor on important political matters. From time to time Howe even appeared in FDR's place when Roosevelt couldn't attend an event. Howe was a tough critic, yet supported FDR at every point in his career, deferring to FDR as "The Boss" and dedicating most of his life to Roosevelt.

Some say Howe had too much control over Roosevelt, while others claimed he mentored him well and advised him against making some giant political mistakes. Eleanor Roosevelt was also very close to Howe, who coached her in public speaking and encouraged her to embark upon her own political career. She called him "one of the seven most important people" in her life.

FDR worked tirelessly to defeat Sheehan's bid for senator. Even at his relatively young age, Franklin was able to attract other Democrats to his way of thinking, and eventually, the party bosses withdrew Sheehan's name from consideration. Though Shepard was not selected, FDR's efforts ensured that another candidate, Justice James A. O'Gorman, was sent to the Senate.

The fact that FDR was able to influence party politics so early in his career proved that he was a force to be reckoned with. By 1912, FDR's opinion held some weight in political circles. It was a presidential election year, and FDR supported Democratic candidate Woodrow Wilson. It was important to FDR to be loyal to the Democratic Party even though his cousin Theodore Roosevelt was running as a third-party candidate.

A Political Error

In 1914, FDR decided to run in the Democratic primary for the U.S. Senate seat from New York. It was a last-minute decision, made because FDR felt that the Democratic Party bosses could not put up a respectable candidate. He assumed incorrectly, however—the party bosses found a good candidate in former U.S. ambassador to Germany James W. Gerard. Gerard won by a margin of three to one, and FDR learned that a candidate needed to be sure of his support in order to win elections.

FDR's loyalty was rewarded. After Wilson was inaugurated on March 4, 1913, he appointed FDR to the post of assistant secretary of the navy. FDR was thrilled with the appointment, especially since Theodore Roosevelt had once held the same position. His enthusiasm was clear in a letter he wrote on March 17, 1913: "I am baptized, confirmed, sworn in, vaccinated—and somewhat at sea! For over an hour I have been signing papers, which had to be accepted on faith—but I hope luck will keep me out of jail. I will have to work like a new turbine to master this job—but it will be done if it takes all summer."

Naval Life

During his tenure in the navy, FDR was in charge of many things, including civilian personnel, relations between the navy and civilian officials, and preparing the navy's budgets. He said of his job, "I get my fingers into everything and there's no law against it."

His demanding position meant spending a great deal of time away from his family, but Franklin tried to be as good a father as he could. Every summer, the Roosevelts left Washington to vacation on Campobello Island, where Franklin hiked, sailed, and swam with his children. Franklin's son James later wrote, "We spent so little time alone with our parents, that those times are treasured as though gifts from the gods. Father loved life on the island more than any of us, but got to spend the least time there. . . . Father taught us to sail. This was the one activity he loved above all others and wanted us to love." Franklin even used the perks of his position for his family's benefit from time to time. In 1916, when a polio outbreak threatened New York City, Franklin persuaded the navy to let him send a naval ship to transport his children from the end of their vacation in Maine back to Hyde Park. Polio is a contagious viral disease, and Franklin made these arrangements so that his children could avoid traveling through any areas that might be infected. The ship brought the children home without risk of exposure to the disease.

Franklin very much enjoyed his position as assistant secretary of the U.S. Navy. Here, he pins the Medal of Honor on Lieutenant Commander Joel T. Boone.

Mostly, FDR worked hard during his years as assistant secretary of the navy advocating for Woodrow Wilson. He did, however, disagree with Wilson's policies on occasion. After

The *Lusitania*, an American cruise ship, was sunk by a German submarine in 1915, leading FDR to question President Wilson's policy of neutrality during the early years of World War I.

Germany declared war on Russia on August 1, 1914, FDR wanted the United States to join what was to become World War I to help Russia. He told Eleanor, "A complete smash-up is inevitable. It will be the greatest war in the world's history." FDR was greatly frustrated when Wilson declared that the country would stay neutral.

When a German submarine attacked and sank a cruise ship named the *Lusitania* on May 7, 1915, FDR again hoped that the United States would join the war. He felt that the *Lusitania* attack was enough to draw the United States into the conflict, but Wilson once again disagreed. Wilson declared three days later that the United States was "too proud to fight" and would not join the British, French, and other Allied forces against Germany. FDR seethed at the news and was hard-pressed to support this stance. He lamented in 1915 to Eleanor, "I just *know* I shall do some awful unneutral thing before I get through!"

A First Taste of War

Finally, on April 2, 1917, President Wilson went to Congress to announce the U.S. entry into the war. He said, "It is a fearful thing to lead this great peaceful people into the most terrible and disastrous of all wars. . . ." The president felt that the cause of defending peace in the world as well as the principles America was founded on was worth our country's wealth and resources and even the lives of its citizens.

Army recruitment posters featuring Uncle Sam, such as this one, first appeared during World War I. The artist, James Montgomery Flagg, used his own face as a model for Uncle Sam, adding white hair and a beard.

First Call
I Need <u>You</u> in the <u>Navy</u> this Minute!
Our Country will always be proudest of those who answered the FIRST CALL

Navy Recruiting Stations:
34 East 23rd Street   115 Flatbush Ave.
New York   Brooklyn

When the United States entered World War I, FDR wanted to resign from the navy and enlist in the armed forces. Wilson, however, rejected his resignation. Instead of fighting on the field of battle, FDR spent the war inspecting overseas naval bases and conferring with Allied leaders. As Roosevelt biographer James MacGregor Burns wrote, "The war years had a maturing effect on Roosevelt. Long hours, tough decisions, endless conferences, exhausting trips, hard bargaining with powerful officials in Washington and abroad turned him into a seasoned politician-administrator." This experience would serve FDR well in the years to come, as his star continued to rise.

CHAPTER 4

Tragedy and Triumph

I would rather be right than Vice President.

World War I drew to a close after Germany surrendered on November 11, 1918, and the peace process began in 1919. FDR was involved in various aspects of ending the war, and remained loyal to President Wilson through the remainder of his tenure as assistant secretary of the navy. Even though FDR stayed loyal to the president, the rest of the country was moving away from Wilson. People began to associate the president with government controls, high taxes, and, most of all, a world war that had lost public support by its close. All of this caused FDR to plan his next political move. He needed to prove to the American people that he was his own man, separate from the president.

During the 1920 election year, the Democratic Party met in San Francisco, California, for its convention and nominated James M. Cox, a three-time governor of Ohio, for president. Cox decided on FDR as a running mate. At the young age of thirty-eight, FDR had been nominated for the office of vice president of the United States. FDR wrote after the convention: "The action at San Francisco was the greatest possible surprise to me, and has entirely upset my plans for a peaceful summer! If things go through on November 2nd, I am going to make an effort to put the job of Vice-President on the map for the first time in history."

FDR was the running mate of presidential candidate James M. Cox, shown here to the right of FDR. Their bid was unsuccessful.

Despite FDR's best campaign efforts, however, he and Cox lost the election by more than 7 million votes—the Republican victory by Warren G. Harding was one of the most sweeping wins in presidential history. FDR accepted defeat but immediately made plans for the future. After all, the experience had not been a total waste. FDR was now known throughout the United States and had made a great deal of invaluable contacts he could call upon in coming years.

A Life-Changing Illness

After losing his bid for vice president, FDR found himself unemployed. He no longer had his naval appointment and did not hold public office. FDR returned to his law practice and took a job as vice president of the Fidelity and Deposit Company of Maryland, in charge of the company's New York office.

In the summer of 1921, Franklin's life changed forever. That August, the Roosevelts were on vacation in Campobello. On August 8, Franklin slipped and fell off the deck of his boat. That night, he suffered a bit of a chill but felt well enough the next day to resume his normal vacation schedule. Franklin went for a swim, ran for two miles, and jumped into the ice-cold waters of the Bay of Fundy. At the end of all this activity, Franklin again felt ill and went to bed.

In the morning, Franklin's back and legs ached, and he had a high fever. Eleanor wrote on August 14, "We have had a few very anxious days. Wednesday evening, Franklin was taken ill. By Friday evening, he lost the ability to walk or move his legs. The doctor feels sure he will get well, but it may take some time." Franklin later described his experience: "I tried to persuade myself that the trouble with my leg was muscular, that it would disappear as I used it, but presently it refused to work, and then the other."

Polio

Polio, which is also called poliomyelitis or infantile paralysis, is a contagious disease caused by a virus. The disease damages the central nervous system and can cause paralysis and muscle weakness. There is no treatment for polio; and before the development of a vaccine for this disease, polio affected as many as 57,000 Americans a year.

Dr. Jonas Salk, whose work would lead to a vaccine effective in the prevention of polio.

Franklin's first two doctors misdiagnosed his illness as either a cold or a blood clot. Finally, after two weeks, a third doctor had the right diagnosis, though it was crushing news. Franklin had polio, which was rampant across the northeast that summer. It had taken hold of his body and paralyzed his legs. As a true Roosevelt, Franklin did not complain and tried to convince everyone that everything was going to be fine. He was especially careful to be cheerful in front of his mother. Privately, however, he was terrified. He even asked a good friend why God had deserted him.

For weeks, Franklin was flat on his back in bed, unable to move. His body temperature was either very high or abnormally low. In mid-September, Franklin was finally able to travel to New York, where he spent six weeks in the hospital. Doctors noted that Franklin could move his toes, but he could not extend his feet or sit up on his own. When Franklin was sent home at the end of October, his medical report indicated that he was not getting any better.

FDR relaxing in Warm Springs, Georgia, 1923. FDR felt that the natural spring water soothed his polio symptoms, so he made frequent trips to the town and later established a polio treatment center there.

It took many years for Franklin to fully accept that he would never walk without help again and that his progress—even across a room—would be slow. He had firmly believed that he would leave the hospital on crutches but walking on his own. When that didn't happen, he told friends

FDR (far right, seated), shown here with the crew of his yacht, *The Larooco*, was able to enjoy the outdoors in spite of his disability.

that he was certain he would soon walk on crutches and eventually walk with only canes. He searched for a cure with doctors all over the country, continuing the search until the final days of his life.

In 1924, a few years after contracting the illness, Franklin, along with his friend John S. Lawrence, bought a houseboat called *The Larooco*. Franklin headed south to Florida where he could swim, fish, and relax with friends. He wanted the sun and the exercise, but he also wanted a break from his mother and wife and their attentions. Franklin used the time to grieve for his loss. One of Franklin's friends remembered: "There were days on *The Larooco* when it was noon before he could pull himself out of depression and greet his guests, wearing his light-hearted facade."

Six years after his bout with polio, Franklin wrote to one of his doctors: "My own legs continue to improve [but] I cannot get rid of that brace on the left leg yet. It is still a mystery as to why that left knee declines to lock."

Making Adjustments

Franklin began regular physical therapy sessions, which were painful and exhausting. An important part of his therapy included frequent trips to the spring water pools at Warm Springs, Georgia. Franklin felt that the naturally warm water helped in the treatment and rehabilitation of polio victims who required supported exercise.

In February 1922, Franklin was fitted for the leg braces he would wear for the rest of his life. They were seven-pound contraptions made of leather and steel that extended from his hips to his feet. The braces locked at the knees, turning his legs into stiff stilts. With these braces in place, Franklin began the process of learning to walk again.

Adjusting to the realities of life after polio was necessary for all of the Roosevelts. FDR's children also had to learn to deal with their father's condition, and Franklin did his best to make the transition easy for them. When his son James returned from Groton for Christmas, he was nervous about seeing his father. James later wrote: "His chin still stuck out and he was grinning and he stretched out his arms to me. 'Come here, old man,' he said. I rushed over and received his embrace. . . . Then though I was a Roosevelt and a Grotonian, I cried a bit, but, with Pa

Politics in the Family

During his years in Washington, FDR laid the groundwork for his political career. He went to parties and met with all the right people. He could not, however, convince Eleanor to enjoy herself in the Washington whirlwind. Eleanor actually described her life as being caught in the slavery of the Washington social system, where her only duty was to advance her husband's career. She later wrote, "I was perfectly certain that I had nothing to offer, and that my duty as the wife of a public official was to do exactly as the majority of women were doing."

squeezing me and slapping me on the back and carrying on enthusiastically . . . I soon was chattering along with him." Still, there were hard times as well, while Franklin wrestled with his own fears and anger over his condition. He often tended to build walls between himself and his loved ones. James also wrote: "These were the lonely years. We had no tangible father, no father whom we could touch and talk to, only a cheery letter-writer."

In light of his new disabilities, Franklin's focus shifted away from politics for a while. At the time, paralysis had a certain amount of shame attached to it—so-called good families kept their disabled relatives out of sight. These victims of disease were dismissed as cripples and were thought to be unable to contribute to society. In fact, after Franklin got out of the hospital, Sara had wanted him to go home with her to Hyde Park where she could nurse him. He could pursue his hobbies; but a political career, she thought, was out of the question. Eleanor saved Franklin from the fate of a forgotten invalid. She supported his hopes to one day return to political life, saying: "I don't want him forgotten. . . . I want him to have a voice."

FDR slowly returned to some public activities, like his law practice

Roosevelt's leg braces can be seen in this photograph.

and charity fund-raising. He wrote political articles for various publications and commented from time to time on the state of politics. In October 1921, when asked for his favorite motto, FDR could not help but answer with a criticism of the current presidential administration. FDR took the opportunity to make it plain he felt the president, Warren G. Harding was short on the ability to make international policies that would maintain worldwide peace. He said, "I will be justified in giving this as my favorite motto: 'I would rather be right than Vice President.' "

"I don't want him forgotten. . . . I want him to have a voice."

Back in the Game

By 1924, FDR's political ambitions had resurfaced, though he was not ready to face an election as a candidate. He was able to reenter politics, thanks in large part to his wife's efforts, while he recuperated physically and mentally from his illness. Eleanor, in a sense, had become Franklin's link to the world of politics. At first, Eleanor was intimidated by politics, but she soon learned that she had quite a bit of skill. She kept FDR in touch with important officials and influential thinkers, arranging introductions and meetings when needed. Eleanor also became politically active as an editor of the *Women's Democratic News*; and she turned the women's division of the New York State Democratic Party into a serious political force. She even managed to have women appointed as delegates to the state convention. Within a few years, she had become a voice for those who had none, championing reform causes such as child labor laws, public housing, workers' compensation, and unemployment insurance.

FDR had spent his years away from public office developing good relationships with powerful politicians, especially with New York governor Alfred E. Smith. Smith played a large role in FDR's political comeback. At the time, Smith had his eye on the White House. FDR and Smith exchanged letters, with FDR offering his political advice. Their friendship made FDR the second most powerful Democrat in the state of New York.

When the 1924 Democratic National Convention rolled around, Smith asked his friend FDR to nominate him for president. FDR agreed. On June 26, at noon, FDR made his public debut nine years after his bout with polio.

The biggest goal of this appearance was to prove to the public that FDR was not hopelessly disabled. FDR carefully practiced how he would walk up to the stage. He wanted to minimize the audience's shock when first seeing his condition, and he certainly never wanted to appear as an invalid. By

The Great Depression affected both farmers and city dwellers. In this photograph, unemployed men in Washington, D.C., wait in line at a Volunteers of American soup kitchen.

grasping one of his sons' upper arms on his left and holding a crutch in his right hand, FDR developed a technique of hitching his legs forward from the hip. He instructed his son, "You must not let people see that this is difficult or takes effort or it hurts." To distract the audience from his difficult progress, he chatted excitedly with his son and made eye contact with nearby observers. Once at the stage, FDR then took a second crutch and climbed to the podium on his own.

The auditorium erupted in applause as the twenty thousand people there rose to give FDR a standing ovation.

FDR had to cover a distance of only fifteen feet, but during his approach, everyone in the auditorium was completely silent. He dragged his useless legs inch by inch, supported by his son James, determined to reach the stage. When FDR arrived at the podium, he was sweating, and it was obvious to everyone that he had been concentrating hard on the task at hand. However, he immediately threw his head and shoulders back and gave the audience his distinctive broad smile. The auditorium erupted in applause as the twenty thousand people there rose to give FDR a standing ovation. The applause lasted for several minutes.

FDR's speech was rousing, and it was easily the most memorable part of the convention. Smith did not receive the nomination but was grateful for FDR's efforts nonetheless. Smith ran again in 1928 and again asked FDR to nominate him. The goal for FDR was, once more, to show that he was a viable political candidate, not just a polio victim. Before the convention, Eleanor wrote to FDR to say: "I'm telling everyone you're going to Houston without crutches." This time, FDR used his son Elliott's help and a cane rather than a crutch. When he reached the

FDR addresses an Al Smith rally at Madison Square Garden. Smith was the first Roman Catholic presidential candidate representing a major political party.

podium, a reporter commented, "Here on the stage is Franklin Roosevelt, a figure tall and proud even in suffering, pale with years of struggle against paralysis, a man softened and cleansed and illumined with pain. For the moment we are lifted up."

Smith gave FDR something more politically valuable than exposure at a national convention—he encouraged FDR to run for governor of New York and supported his campaign. FDR had finally recovered, in a sense, from his illness—though he could not walk unassisted, he was once again destined to be a political force.

CHAPTER 5

Governor and Beyond

I am a disciple in a great cause.

Although FDR was very driven to succeed at politics, it took some convincing to get him to run for governor. For a long time, he wanted to put off political aspirations until he could walk again. He soon realized, though, that his aspirations would have to move forward without his legs.

Still, after Smith began campaigning for president, he had to repeatedly telephone FDR to try to convince him to run. FDR put on elaborate ruses to avoid even taking Smith's phone calls. When his daughter, Anna, expressed to FDR that she felt he should run, he responded, "You ought to be spanked."

FDR hadn't even agreed to run when the New York State convention delegates successfully nominated him for governor. He accepted then with good grace, saying, "I am a disciple in a great cause. . . . I cannot fail to heed a call to . . . active service in a time when so much is at stake."

Al Smith strongly encouraged FDR (seated) to run for governor of New York.

The Campaign and the Disability

As in the past with other elections, FDR campaigned enthusiastically for governor. In order to be elected, he knew that he had to gain the support of an array of ethnic groups in the melting pot that was New York City as well as in the rest of the state. The votes of Catholics, Jews, and African Americans could make the difference for either candidate. Therefore, FDR spoke out about the discrimination that many groups experienced at that time. In a speech in Binghamton, New York, on October 17, 1928, FDR said, "I believe that the day will come in this country when education . . . will be so widespread, so clean, so American, that [discrimination] . . . will not be able to survive." This tactic endeared him to many of the voters who also disagreed with discrimination.

FDR tried to appeal to the working class, as well, especially factory workers and farmers. He supported limits on the number of hours women or children could legally work, saying that he disagreed with his opposition's view that it was up to an employer as to how long a person worked or how much the employer paid. He also supported an old-age pension, something that workers at that time did not normally get.

Despite improvements in child labor laws, the Depression made it necessary for many children to work in the family business. Here, a young Indiana boy weaves a rug in the Emvich family farmhouse.

Child Labor

Until the early twentieth century, children worked in factories, fields, mines, and mills, as well as in a variety of other physically demanding and dangerous jobs. Because they were cheap to employ—some children worked seventy hours a week for only pennies—companies were happy to hire them. Most of these children's families were so poor that they needed even the small change that the children could bring home.

The child laborers began work at as young as five years of age. They usually did not attend school. Their health suffered from the work. Poor ventilation in factories caused lung diseases such as bronchitis and tuberculosis. In mines, children injured themselves carrying heavy loads of coal on their backs. In glass factories, children cut themselves on shards of glass and burned themselves at the furnaces. Accidents with machinery led to the loss of fingers, eyesight, and even lives.

People began to protest against child labor in the early 1900s, Eleanor Roosevelt being among the strongest critics. Still, it was very difficult to eliminate the practice. Even during the Great Depression when millions of adults had lost their jobs, children were still working in the same horrible conditions. It was not until 1938 that a law was passed that set age limits on workers and limited the types of jobs children could hold.

Even though he had run for office before, this campaign posed new challenges for FDR. This election was the first time he was asking Americans to vote for him despite his disability. FDR's physical limitations did create a number of difficulties during his campaign. When FDR gave speeches, he could not always climb the stairs up to the meeting halls. He often had to be carried up fire escapes or back stairs. FDR did not sulk because he needed help in this way. Rather, as his colleague Frances Perkins noted, "He came up over that perilous, uncomfortable, and humiliating 'entrance,' and his manner was pleasant, courteous, enthusiastic. He got up on his own braces, adjusted them, straightened himself, smoothed his hair, linked his arm in his son Jim's, and walked out on the platform as if this were nothing unusual."

The Republicans felt that FDR's disability meant that he was not a serious candidate. FDR, however, did everything he could to counter that opinion. On October 28, 1928, FDR said in a speech in Troy, New York, that after he received the Democratic nomination for governor, "there was a great deal of . . . sob stuff among the Republican editorial writers in the state of New York. They said, 'Isn't it too bad that that unfortunate man has had to be drafted for the Governorship? Isn't it too bad that his health won't stand it?'" He then went on to describe his two-week campaign tour that covered 190 miles by automobile and during which he made seven speeches. In 1928, it took days to travel this kind of distance in a car, so by traveling long distances and keeping to tough schedules, FDR proved that he was strong enough for the job.

> "He came up over that perilous, uncomfortable, and humiliating 'entrance,' and his manner was pleasant, courteous, enthusiastic."

FDR had a lot of support from his friends, who gave more weight to his abilities than to his disability. Alfred Smith answered the Republican charge that FDR could not physically handle the governorship by saying, "We don't elect a Governor for his ability to do a double back flip or a handspring. The work of the Governorship is brainwork." FDR also had an agreement with the press—no reporter was allowed to take photographs of FDR being assisted in and out of cars, carried up or down stairs, or during any other activity that would highlight his disability and alarm the voters. This agreement was never violated.

Election Day

When FDR had been nominated for New York State governor, the general public believed that he would not win. Republicans were expecting a presidential win and also the New York State governorship. By the beginning of November, however, the odds seemed to have evened out. Some people even suspected that FDR had a slight edge.

On November 6, Roosevelt and his campaign team gathered at his headquarters in the Biltmore Hotel in New York City to track the results of the election races all around the country. Early on, it was clear that Smith was not going to be elected president. In fact, it even looked like Smith was going to lose New York.

FDR had a lot of support from his friends, who gave more weight to his abilities than to his disability.

FDR's own race was much closer. Republican election officials in upstate New York had a reputation for holding back results from their districts until they could gauge their party's needs, possibly to change the results to help their candidates win. Therefore, FDR and his team telephoned area sheriffs to warn that a "staff of a hundred lawyers" was prepared to seek out election fraud, should there be any. The calls went late into the night to prevent any election tampering. The election results did not come in until around four o'clock the next morning.

The final tally was 2,104,629 votes for FDR's opponent, Albert Ottinger, and 2,130,193 votes for Roosevelt. FDR had won by a margin of a little more than 25,000 votes. The election win not only gave FDR the governorship of New York State, but because of Smith's loss, it had also made FDR the country's most important Democrat.

New York Politics

At noon on January 1, 1929, FDR was sworn in as the governor of New York. He said that day that he hoped his election would herald an "Era of Good Feeling" between different political groups. He hoped that the Democrats and Republicans in the state legislature could put aside their differences to work toward common goals. During the course of his first term, however, FDR ran into opposition from the legislature over such issues as tax relief for farmers, the state budget, the public ownership of electricity, funding for state hospitals, and social reform bills.

FDR lost more than his fair share of these battles with the legislature. Still, his first term was considered successful, and he was reelected to office in 1930 by a much larger margin than he had won by in 1928. In addition,

"I cast that one vote!"

FDR won his second term as governor of New York by a record margin— more than 750,000 votes—almost doubling Smith's record-breaking margin of 387,000 votes years before. Some tallies had him winning by 750,001 votes, at which FDR's typical sense of humor took over. He said, "I cast that one vote!"

Al Smith, center left, and Roosevelt, center right, tip their hats to the crowd at FDR's inauguration as governor of the state of New York in January 1929.

FDR used his time as governor to learn how to better move through the world of politics. To counter the Republican-influenced press in New York, he began to give Fireside Chats. These chats were live radio addresses given in a friendly tone. Those listening imagined he was talking to them from beside a fireplace in his home.

The broadcasts gave the public an opportunity to hear Roosevelt's views without editing or commentary from Republican news reporters. The chats also allowed him to reach people who may have been biased against a Democrat and to try to sway them on a more personal basis. He said later, "I find that radio has made it possible for the average citizen to get firsthand information, and that, in the long run, is bound to result in better understanding of general problems in government."

Roosevelt had been re-elected as governor of New York, but had his sights set even higher beyond that win. As early as 1928, FDR had confessed to a friend and adviser, "I believe I can be nominated for the Presidency in 1932 on the Democratic ticket."

★ ★ ★ ★ ★ ★ ★ ★ ★ ★ ★ ★ ★ ★ ★ ★

On the Radio

In 1924, fewer than 5 percent of American families owned a radio. By 1932, more than 60 percent of homes and 250,000 cars had radios. The technology was catching on all over the nation.

FDR, in particular, understood the importance of using the radio to communicate with large numbers of people. He was a pioneer in turning the radio into a political tool. For well over a decade, radio was the most important technology for transmitting the news to the public—as important then as television and Internet news coverage are today.

By 1932, radio was bringing entertainment aimed at each member of the family into most American homes. For the first time, politicians like FDR could speak to American citizens directly.

CHAPTER 6

Rise to the Presidency

This is the greatest night of my life.

F DR was riding a huge wave of support in New York by 1932, but it was national events—specifically national misfortunes—that made it possible for him to run for president. Twelve years earlier, in 1920, Democrats had lost the White House to Warren G. Harding. One reason that voters had moved away from President Wilson's Democratic Party was the economic slump that the country was experiencing in the early 1920s. The economy turned around under successive Republican presidents Harding and Calvin Coolidge, and Americans experienced great prosperity. By the late 1920s, however, during Republican Herbert Hoover's term, another economic depression had settled over the country. This slump was called the Great Depression. It was worse than any previous depression, mainly because of the stock market crash on October 29, 1929, a day now known as "Black Tuesday."

The Depression Begins

A stock market is a place where people can buy or sell portions (called "stocks") of businesses as investments. As the value of a business increases, so does the money earned by people who own the stock. But when the stock market crashes, the value of the stocks plummets dramatically. Investments lose value, and people lose money. On Black

Tuesday, the stock market lost almost one-fifth of its total value. Between October 29 and November 13, the day when stock prices hit their lowest point, an estimated $22–40 billion vanished from the American economy. This figure is comparable to the total amount spent by the United States fighting in World War I.

Many people lost all the money they had in the stock market crash. Worse, however, was that some banks had been investing in the stock market as well—but the money the banks were using was pooled from their customers' savings. When the stock market crashed, the banks lost their investments and therefore lost their customers' money. As more and more people tried to withdraw their money, the banks did not have enough cash to cover the withdrawals. This situation had a snowball effect. Upon

The New York Stock Exchange has seen many ups and downs since its founding in 1817.

hearing that some people couldn't get their money out of their banks, others panicked and rushed to withdraw their funds. Soon, banks had little or no money to operate with, and when the money ran out, the banks had to close, sometimes indefinitely. By the winter of 1932, the U.S. banking system had nearly collapsed.

The Roaring Twenties screeched to a halt as people found themselves out of work. Breadlines, like the one shown here in New York City, were often run by charities and helped feed the most destitute.

By March 1933, more than five thousand banks had failed and millions of people lost their savings.

Soon, people were desperate for a job—any job. Homeless people filled the streets of major cities. Breadlines and soup lines formed everywhere. Said New Yorker Bill Bailey, "I couldn't find a job. I'd get out and maybe hustle fifteen places a day—banging on warehouse doors, stuff like that. Impossible. I ended up selling apples. . . . In New York City there was nothing that struck the imagination more than seeing a soup line of 500 people. Then two days later, 1,000 people in the same line. And it kept on growing and growing." The hungry and homeless were even camped out within a few blocks of the Roosevelts' townhouse in New York City. Eleanor told the townhouse's cook to provide hot coffee and sandwiches to any person who came to the door hungry.

From the governor's office in New York, FDR watched these national events unfold. As the Depression began to affect the economy of his own state, FDR took action. In March 1930, he created an emergency unemployment committee to explore ways to keep employment levels high. Later that year, FDR took steps to expand public works and provide government relief to those in need. In August 1931, FDR persuaded the legislature to create the Temporary Emergency Relief Administration, which set aside $20 million to tide over New Yorkers during the winter of 1931.

"The country needs . . . bold, persistent experimentation."

In addition to helping those in need, FDR was laying the groundwork for a campaign for president. In his speeches and writings, he began to condemn President Hoover's administration for lack of leadership during the Depression. He said: "The country needs . . . bold, persistent experimentation. It is common sense to take a method and try it; if it fails, admit it frankly and try another. But above all, try something."

The Fight for the Nomination

On January 22, 1932, FDR wrote a letter to the state Democratic Committee of North Dakota to have his name placed on the ballot for the state's presidential primary. This was his first official step toward the presidency.

The field of Democratic candidates, however, was quite crowded in 1932. The Great Depression was hurting the incumbent president, and Democrats felt that they could win the White House. FDR was the favored candidate early on, but there were half a dozen other serious candidates, including Alfred Smith. FDR's friend had now become his opponent. The Democratic National Convention of 1932 was held in Chicago in the summer. Although FDR wasn't even present at the convention, he went in as the favorite to win, but it was difficult to gain the

Franklin (seated, left), campaigning for president in his home state of New York in 19xx along with his running mate, John Garner (seated, right).

two-thirds majority needed to get the nomination. The first ballot gave FDR 664¼ votes, compared to Smith's 201¾, as well as a handful of votes for the other two main candidates. A second ballot increased FDR's tally to 677¾, but this number was still 91 votes shy of the nomination.

With momentum on his side, it soon became clear to the delegates that FDR would win. The voting began to shift. By the fourth ballot, the California delegation voted for FDR. The next largest delegations, from Illinois and Texas, also cast their votes for FDR. Soon, FDR—and his newly named running mate, John Garner—had amassed 945 votes, about 150 more than they needed. The chairman of the convention, Senator Thomas Walsh of Montana, declared FDR the nominee at 10:32 p.m. on July 1. FDR's victory ended any friendship or political partnership with Alfred Smith. There was no time to dwell on Smith, however. FDR had much on his mind as Walsh declared him the nominee. For one thing, he still had to win over many Democrats nationwide. One politician was overheard lamenting, "It's a kangaroo ticket.

Stronger in the hindquarter than in front." Also, as Walsh announced to the delegates, for the first time in American history, the nominee would address the convention the day after receiving the nomination for president of the United States.

The New Deal Is Proposed

FDR arrived in Chicago on July 2, 1932, with Eleanor and his children, as well as an entourage of secretaries and security men. His speech to the convention began shortly after 7 p.m.

FDR faced a huge challenge. He needed to lay out a plan that would both balance the federal government's budget and provide financial relief to the millions of Americans suffering because of the Depression. Just as during other key moments in his life, FDR was outwardly calm and serene—he even managed to nap on the plane while his family shivered on the chilly flight and his son John was airsick. Still, he was reworking the speech up until the last moment, even rewriting it during the car ride to the convention center. The result was historic.

FDR said: "The greatest tribute I can pay to my countrymen is that in these days of crushing

A New Deal Myth

Many historians and prominent Roosevelt biographers have reported that Rollin Kirby's famous political cartoon actually showed a plane with the words "New Deal" written on the underside of the wings. It is unclear where this mistake originated, but this description is not true. The words New Deal were not yet popular enough for Kirby to use on his plane. In fact, they did not become a popular catch phrase until after Kirby's cartoon was published.

want there persists an orderly and hopeful spirit on the part of millions of our people who have suffered so much. To fail to offer them a new chance is not only to betray their hopes but to misunderstand their patience. . . . This is no time for fear. . . . The main issue of this campaign should revolve about the clear fact of our economic condition, a depression so deep that it is without precedent in modern history. . . . My program is based upon this moral principle: The welfare and soundness of a Nation depend first upon what the great mass of the people wish and need; and second, whether or not they are getting it. . . . I pledge you, I pledge myself to a new deal for the American people." In response, the convention erupted into cheers.

The next day, a political cartoon by Rollin Kirby showed a farmer gazing up at an airplane in the sky with the word "Roosevelt" written on the wings and FDR's "new deal" pledge on a flyer floating downward. Soon, the term *New Deal* became the popular way to describe FDR's proposals.

Race to Election Day

During the campaign, FDR kept hammering his opponent, President Herbert Hoover, on his record. On October 19 in a speech in Pittsburgh, Pennsylvania, he criticized

FDR with his son, James, on the Presidential Special. Note that Franklin, left, is holding onto James's arm in order to wave to the crowd while standing.

On the Eve of Election

The night before the 1932 election, as his son James helped him into bed, Franklin made a confession. James wrote, "All the years I knew him, there was only one time when Father worried about his ability. It was the night he was elected President. 'You know, Jimmy,' he said to me, 'all my life, I have been afraid of only one thing, fire. Tonight I think I'm afraid of something else.' 'Afraid of what, Father?' I asked. 'I'm afraid that I may not have the strength to do the job.' " Franklin resolved to pray for strength and asked James to pray for him as well. It was a large responsibility—Americans and the world were now looking to FDR to bring the United States out of the Depression and into a new era of prosperity.

the president for spending unnecessary money on government offices and commissions. FDR campaigned like this all over the country, approaching this election as enthusiastically as any of the previous ones. He traveled more than 13,000 miles by train and gave sixteen major speeches and sixty-seven **stump speeches** during his presidential campaign.

Part of FDR's charm on the campaign trail was his instinctive understanding of how to bond with his audience. At almost every stop on his train tour, FDR would smile at the gathering crowd and announce that he was glad to be back—he did this whether he'd been there before or not. Next, FDR would tell everyone that he was there to listen to their concerns. He would also introduce his family members who were traveling with him, especially his son James who had, as FDR almost always said, "less hair than I do." (Apparently, James quickly tired of his father's comedy routine, although that didn't stop FDR.) Then, of course, the train would start to move again and FDR would leave, without actually having listened to anyone—and yet, the performance worked.

As hard as FDR campaigned, Hoover campaigned for re-election just as hard. Unfortunately for Hoover, however, his speeches were considered bleak and hopeless. Once, someone in Hoover's audiences commented that the president was so depressing that, "if you put a rose in Hoover's hand, it would wilt." Hoover offered no plan for change; rather, he insisted there was nothing for the country to do but plod onward on the course he had determined in his first term. Considering the mood of the American people, this strategy had no hope of winning.

Election Day proved to be far less suspenseful than many of FDR's previous experiences. Early in the night, it was obvious FDR had won. The final tally showed he received 22,821,857 votes to Hoover's 15,761,841. FDR received 57 percent of the popular vote, 472 **electoral votes**, and had won forty-two states. He confessed to his mother, "This is the greatest night of my life."

Turmoil in Her Heart and Mind

As exhilarating as the election victory was for FDR, it was equally troubling for Eleanor. She wrote, "I was happy for my husband. I knew that it would make up for the blow that fate had dealt him when he was stricken with infantile paralysis. . . . But for myself, I was deeply troubled. . . . [T]his meant the end of any personal life of my own. . . . The turmoil in my heart and mind was rather great that night."

CHAPTER 7

The New Deal in Action

*This great Nation will endure as it has endured,
will revive and will prosper. . . . [T]he only thing
we have to fear is fear itself.*

Though FDR won the election, he had to wait until
March of 1933 to take office. During the months
between Election Day and FDR's inauguration, Hoover
attempted to tell FDR the steps he should take as
president. FDR, however, refused to get involved in joint
decisions with the outgoing president.

An Assassination Attempt

To steer clear of Hoover altogether, FDR decided to go
on a cruise off the coast of Florida. Before leaving, he gave
a short speech in Miami on February 15, 1933. He was
joined at the speech by the mayor of Chicago, Anton
Cermak.

As was FDR's habit, he gave the speech perched on
the back of his open car, which was easier than trying to
maneuver himself up to a podium. During the speech, a
man named Giuseppe Zangara tried to assassinate FDR.
He fired six shots in FDR's direction while balancing on a
wobbly wooden chair. From his unsteady position,
Zangara hit Cermak instead of FDR. Cermak died of his
wounds two weeks later.

Giuseppe Zangara

Giuseppe Zangara was an Italian immigrant who became a naturalized citizen of the United States. He worked as a bricklayer, but he was driven mad by constant pain in his abdomen. He somehow came to believe that the president was causing his pain through supernatural means. He first plotted to kill Herbert Hoover but did not want to travel to Washington where the cold weather worsened his abdominal pain. When he heard that FDR was speaking in Miami, Zangara decided to assassinate him instead, because "Hoover and Roosevelt—everybody the same."

Two weeks after the assassination attempt, on March 20, 1933, Zangara was executed in the electric chair at Florida State Penitentiary after being convicted of Cermak's murder.

The impact of this dangerous episode on FDR is unknown. Immediately after the assassination attempt, FDR thanked the people involved in saving his life. This included Cermak and a Miami housewife named Lillian Cross, who had shoved Zangara's arm, causing the gunman to miss FDR. Then, as far as anyone can remember, FDR never mentioned the incident again.

The Beginning

Despite the unpleasantness of the Zangara episode, most of the reactions to FDR's election were positive. The chief justice of the Supreme Court, Charles Evan Hughes, wrote on February 28 that he hoped that FDR would "have a most successful administration . . . and I especially prize the opportunity of being associated with you in our great American enterprise."

Still, the country was a mess. More than half the states had closed their banks and the New York Stock Exchange had shut down. The entire financial system was about to collapse. Americans focused all of their hope on FDR and what he would do.

On March 3, FDR's train arrived at Union Station in Washington, D.C. He was welcomed by thousands of cheering Americans, eagerly waiting for his inauguration.

At ten o'clock on the morning of March 4, FDR and his family began Inauguration Day by attending a special service at St. John's Episcopal Church. This service was followed by some meetings on the looming financial crisis, and then FDR got into an open car with Hoover to ride to the vice president's inauguration. Finally, at one o'clock, in front of a crowd of 400,000 people, FDR climbed the steps of the Capitol with the help of his son James. Chief Justice Hughes swore him in, and FDR gave a very famous inaugural speech.

"This great Nation will endure as it has endured, will revive and will prosper."

He said: "This great Nation will endure as it has endured, will revive and will prosper. So, first of all, let me assert my firm belief that the only thing we have to fear is fear itself. . . . Our greatest primary task is to put people to work. . . . [W]e require two safeguards against a return of the evils of the old order; there must be a strict supervision of all banking and credits and investments, so that there will be an end to speculation with other people's money; and there must be provision for an adequate but sound currency. These are lines of attack. . . . We cannot merely take but must give as well; that if we are to go forward, we must move as a trained and loyal army willing to sacrifice for the good of a common discipline. . . . I am prepared under my constitutional duty to recommend the measures that a stricken nation in the midst of a stricken world may require. . . . For the trust reposed in me I will return the courage and the devotion that befit the time. I can do no less."

One Hundred Great Days

In his fifteen-minute inaugural speech, FDR called on Americans to join together and to channel their frustrations toward re-creating the nation. The audience was electrified by his words. FDR had touched so many people with his eloquence that he received nearly half a million letters. After the speech, Eleanor commented, "It was very, very solemn, and a little terrifying. The crowds were so tremendous, and you felt that they would do anything—if only someone would tell them what to do."

FDR immediately began working to fix the financial problems of the nation. On March 9, he called a special session of Congress to address those problems. He also declared that day a bank

FDR's first inaugural speech as president, which introduced the phrase "the only thing we have to fear is fear itself." These words would give Americans a small glimpse of hope for the future.

The Brain Trust

As FDR prepared to take office, he assembled a group of advisers, political associates, and correspondents. These people came from a variety of backgrounds and held a range of ideas, but FDR counted on all of them almost equally to weigh in on various problems of the country. They came to be known as the "brain trust"—the people responsible for thinking through solutions for the president.

holiday to prevent more runs on banks and to allow time to reform the banking system.

In the days and weeks that followed, FDR sent a number of bills to Congress to begin the process of recovery. The first was the Emergency Banking Act. This law was designed to give the government the ability to inspect the nation's banks. The Treasury Department became responsible for certifying, or verifying, banks as financially secure. After the banks were certified, they could reopen to consumers. The treasury inspection was designed to help people regain confidence in the banking system. Within three days of the passage of the Emergency Banking Act, five thousand banks had passed inspection and could open their doors again. Over time, even more banks were declared secure.

Later, on June 16, FDR had Congress pass the Banking Act of 1933. This act followed up on the goals of the Emergency Banking Act. One of the most important parts of this act was the creation of the Federal Deposit Insurance Corporation (FDIC). The FDIC was given the authority to regulate and supervise banks in the Federal Reserve System and to provide deposit insurance to banks. This deposit insurance would protect consumers' money even if a bank were to fail. Deposit insurance works in the same way that health insurance pays a person's medical costs or car insurance pays auto repair costs; deposit insurance pays out the money in a person's bank account even if the bank invests it poorly.

FDR was able to end Prohibition—the nationwide ban on alcoholic beverages—by getting Congress to modify the 1919 Volstead Act. This act had prohibited the manufacture, transportation, and sale of beverages containing more than 0.5 percent alcohol. Americans could now manufacture and sell beer and light wines. By establishing a substantial tax on these products, FDR created a large new source of income for the government. FDR was also able to get Congress to establish a number of new federal agencies that would help the country recover from the Great Depression. The Emergency Relief Administration was created to give money to the states for unemployment relief.

FDR created The Civilian Conservation Corps (CCC) to hire millions of unemployed young men between the ages of seventeen and twenty-eight to work on local projects such as planting trees, building wildlife shelters, stocking lakes with fish, and clearing

The New Deal brought work to many who had long been unemployed. These young men are seen working for the CCC in Prince George County, Virginia.

beaches. FDR's plan for this program was to employ young men to restore the country's natural resources. At the same time, these men were taken off the streets and put out into nature. They were also provided with wages they could not earn in any other way in the depressed economy. Between 1933 and 1942, more than 2.5 million young men served in the CCC, where they earned a dollar a day plus clothing and room and board, and where tens of thousands learned to read and write.

The Works Progress Administration (WPA) was also created to provide jobs. The eight million workers in the WPA built hospitals, roads, airports, and schools, among other things. They also translated books into braille so that blind people could read them; made records of spirituals, folk tales, and Native American songs; and interviewed more than two thousand ex-slaves to record their experiences. WPA artists painted murals on public buildings, and WPA actors, singers, and musicians put on plays

The New Deal brought the arts to the public through the Works Progress Administration, as well as providing employment for many artists, musicians, and writers.

The Tennessee Valley Authority was first proposed in the 1920s, but was first set up by FDR in 1933. The TVA helped farmers get the most from their land at a time when such help was sorely needed.

and concerts for millions of Americans, many of whom had never seen a live performance.

The Agricultural Adjustment Administration (AAA) was established to support struggling farmers. Instead of producing huge food surpluses, which drove farm prices down, the AAA raised those prices by paying farmers money to reduce their crop output. The farmers made more money for growing fewer crops. In addition, FDR created the Tennessee Valley Authority (TVA), which hired thousands of people to build dams and power plants along the Tennessee River. The TVA projects provided electricity to many Americans for the first time. The TVA also controlled floods and improved agriculture in one of the poorest parts of the country.

During the first hundred days of FDR's presidency, he was able to push through so much legislation to offer relief to Americans that the period became known as "One Hundred Great Days." Not only did FDR take action through legislation, but he also offered hope and assurances to Americans through his newly re-instated presidential Fireside Chats. As FDR had done while governor of New York, he used these radio broadcasts to address Americans directly, explaining the new government programs, addressing the fears over the banking industry, and reassuring people that the banks were secure. Years later, novelist John Dos Passos said of the Fireside Chats: "People edge their

In his seventh Fireside Chat, FDR talks directly to the American people about the Works Relief Project and the Social Security Act, both of which would change many lives.

chairs up to the radio. There is a man leaning across his desk, speaking clearly and cordially so that you and me will completely understand that he has his fingers on all the switchboards of the federal government."

Protecting His Image

According to historians, Americans did not want to see FDR as handicapped, and FDR was always aware of the need to not look helpless. In the more than forty thousand photographs of FDR that remain at Hyde Park, only two of them show him in a wheelchair, and those are family photos. Every appearance he made as president was carefully planned to keep FDR from looking handicapped.

The Secret Service designed inconspicuous ramps to allow for a wheelchair. Sometimes two agents would support FDR, one on either side. With his arms draped around them, FDR could be carried discreetly.

In preparation for addressing a large crowd, a ramp would be built for FDR's car. He could then merely drive up the ramp and address the crowd while still seated.

To conceal the shiny metal of his leg braces, FDR had them painted black. FDR wore black shoes, black socks, and black trousers cut long, so that the braces all but disappeared.

FDR's shoes were equipped with metal brackets to accommodate his braces.

CHAPTER 8

The Road to Recovery

History probably will record the National Industrial Recovery Act as the most important and far-reaching legislation ever enacted by the American Congress.

Toward the end of the One Hundred Great Days, FDR pushed a piece of legislation called the National Industrial Recovery Act (NIRA) through Congress. This act had two major parts: The first part encouraged companies to work together to increase profits and gave workers the right to bargain as **labor unions** with their employers. The second part created the Public Works Administration to employ up to two million people to build and repair federal buildings, roads, bridges, dams, and other facilities. When the bill was passed, FDR said, "History probably will record the National Industrial Recovery Act as the most important and far-reaching legislation ever enacted by the American Congress. It represents a supreme effort to stabilize for all time the many factors which make for the prosperity of the nation, and the preservation of American standards."

The NIRA allowed FDR, as head of the executive branch of the federal government, to create the National Recovery Administration (NRA). This agency was in charge of encouraging companies to voluntarily agree to industry codes regarding maximum work hours,

A brawny FDR, dressed as a worker and standing center among working men and women, is depicted in this mural by Conrad A. Albrizio. The work was funded by Federal Project Number One, a division of the WPA.

minimum wages, and price fixing. Companies who complied with the NRA's industry codes were allowed to display the Blue Eagle, which became a patriotic symbol. Most companies went along with the NRA for patriotic reasons alone.

By the end of 1933, most Americans were, according to historian Conrad Black, "optimistic that the worst was past and that recovery was in progress." Though many aspects of the New Deal, especially the NIRA, were criticized by many different groups, it seemed that, overall, Americans loved their president.

More Reforms

FDR did not stop with the first round of New Deal programs. In 1934, the Securities and Exchange Act was signed into law to regulate the stock market. This act created the Securities and Exchange Commission (SEC), which made sure that companies provided their investors with truthful financial information and

American Eagle

The NRA Blue Eagle was such a popular symbol that it appeared in shop windows, on posters, and on banners carried in "Blue Eagle" parades. In a show of patriotism, the owner of the professional football team in Philadelphia renamed his team the Eagles in honor of the NRA. That name, the Philadelphia Eagles, is still used by the team today.

General Hugh Johnson, head of the National Recovery Administration, designed the Blue Eagle. The slogan, "We Do Our Part," let customers know that a business complied with the NRA's policies.

that stock brokers put investors' interests first.

While the banking industry was the most important one to reform, FDR felt that the federal government should stay involved in other industry **regulations** as well. The Interstate Commerce Commission was created to handle problems in the transportation industry. FDR also had Congress pass the Federal Power Act of 1935 and the Communications Act. The Federal Power Act gave the Federal Power Commission (FPC) authority to supervise the business deals of electric power companies as well as the transmission of the power. The Communications Act created the Federal Communications Commission (FCC). The FCC was responsible for regulating the radio and telegraph industries, in addition to new technologies as they became available.

When the 1934 congressional elections rolled around, Democrats hoped that FDR's popularity would help win them more seats in Congress. The American public exceeded their expectations. They gave FDR and his New Deal programs a huge vote of confidence by electing many more Democrats than

Republicans. After Election Day, Democrats outnumbered Republicans 322 to 103 in the House of Representatives and 69 to 27 in the Senate. Almost everywhere, the Democratic victories were seen as FDR's victories.

Supreme Woes

In the first part of FDR's term as president, his programs were fairly successful. Though they were criticized by some, on the whole, FDR had support from the country and the government. In 1935, however, a major blow was dealt to FDR's New Deal.

Earlier that year, the Supreme Court declared that a portion of the NIRA, the act that led to the creation of the NRA, was unconstitutional. This decision was followed in May by *Schechter Poultry Corporation v. United States*, otherwise known as the Sick Chicken Case. The four Schechter brothers had a business that sold live chickens to Orthodox Jews in New York. These chickens were prepared for consumption according to Jewish dietary law. The Schechters had been convicted of violating some of the NRA's codes, including one concerning the sale of food that did not meet health standards.

The Bonneville Dam was a New Deal project completed in 1938. The dam brought jobs and energy to the states of Oregon and Washington, as it still does today.

The Supreme Court found that it was unconstitutional for Congress to have given power to set NRA codes—like the live-poultry code—to the executive branch, or the president. The NIRA violated the separation of powers under the U.S. Constitution. In addition, the Supreme Court found that regulating industries like the Schechter Poultry Corporation was the job of the states rather than of the federal government. The NIRA could not regulate such industries.

The NIRA was therefore struck down. As historian Conrad Black described, "the Blue Eagle folded its wings and plunged to earth."

FDR took the decision in fairly good humor and resolved to continue his agenda as best he could. Still, he was clearly upset with the court. In light of the court's decision about state powers and federal powers, FDR wondered out loud, in front of reporters at a press conference on May 31, whether the court believed that the federal government had had the constitutional authority to wage World War I. Comments such as these suggested that FDR was not entirely at ease with the court's actions.

Social Security

There was still overwhelming support for the president from much of the public. Despite the Supreme Court's decision regarding the NIRA, Roosevelt decided to go even further with the New Deal. One major new proposal was Social

Advertisements like this one helped broaden public support for the Social Security Act, which was passed by Congress in 1935.

Security. During the Great Depression, more than 50 percent of American senior citizens had lived in poverty. In 1934, FDR said, "Old age is . . . the most certain, and for many people the most tragic, of all hazards. . . . I hope that in time we may be able to provide . . . a sound and a uniform system which will provide true security." The kind of assistance FDR spoke of—for elderly, unemployed, and disabled people —was common in Europe, Canada, and Australia when FDR became president, but there was no such thing in the United States until the Social Security Act of 1935.

Under FDR's program, the federal government collected money from both employees and employers. These contributions were used to create pensions, or payments for life, for elderly and disabled people. In addition, money was set aside for unemployed workers. They would receive payments from the government while they searched for new jobs.

When FDR signed the Social Security Act into law on August 14, 1935, he said, "This social security measure gives at least some protection to thirty million of our citizens. . . . [W]e have tried to frame a law which will give some measure of protection to the average citizen and to his family against the loss of a job and against poverty-ridden old age."

Because Social Security was not a savings program, elderly Americans were able to begin receiving payments in 1937, a mere two years after the law had passed. That year, more than 53,000 people received benefits.

Though FDR declared the law historic, it was by no means the end of his plans for the country. He assured people that he felt the Social Security Act was one step in a long process. As he approached his second presidential election, FDR made sure that Americans knew his work was not yet done.

CHAPTER 9

A Second Term

*Here in America we are waging
a great and successful war.*

It was 1936, and Franklin Roosevelt's popularity could not have been greater. His first term had created millions of jobs and put the country on the road to recovery. Nevertheless, there were many people who thought that FDR was too extreme and that his programs were turning the United States into a country where citizens were too dependent on the government. Some groups charged that the New Deal was allowing government to interfere with private businesses. Also, many critics condemned the national debt—an amount that had grown to $36 billion by 1936. This debt was almost entirely due to the New Deal's relief programs. Even FDR's former mentor, Alfred Smith, called FDR an irresponsible spender who would bring the country to ruin.

The New Deal was also under attack from an old enemy—the Supreme Court. On January 6, 1936, the court declared the Agricultural Adjustment Administration (AAA) unconstitutional. More decisions followed that further weakened other New Deal programs, especially those that concerned salary and hour regulations for workers. The Court even struck down a New York State minimum-wage law that FDR had enacted as governor. In light of these legal decisions, FDR continued to hint at press conferences that the Supreme Court was overstepping its bounds.

Another Nomination

The concerns voiced by his critics did not weigh as heavily on FDR's mind as did his re-election bid. During the 1936 Democratic Convention, FDR was easily re-nominated by the Democratic Party to run for the presidency. Though he had political opponents, it was clear to anyone who heard the wild cheering and tooting horns or who saw the waving banners and enthusiastic crowds at the convention that FDR was considered by many Americans to be a national hero.

FDR used his nomination acceptance speech to begin his attack on the Supreme Court, an institution that he felt was taking too narrow a view on the issues that faced the nation. He wanted to get the people on his side, so FDR took his case directly to them. He said: What [the justices of the Supreme Court] really complain of is that we seek to take away their power. . . . [H]ere in America we are waging a great and successful war. . . . We are fighting to save a great and precious form of government for ourselves and for the world. I accept the commission you have tendered me. I join with you. I am enlisted for the duration of the war."

Eleanor casts her vote—presumably for her husband—in Hyde Park, New York, in 1936.

Another Win

The campaign itself was no great hardship for FDR. Everywhere he went, cheering crowds waited, eager to get a glimpse of the president. Franklin inspired people with his speeches and his visions for the future. On October 31, 1936, in a speech at Madison Square Garden in New York City, FDR's campaign came to a climax. He ended with the words: "We have only just begun to fight."

On Election Day, almost all those eager voters turned out to cast their ballots for the president. FDR's victory that night was a landslide. He won 523 electoral votes, compared to the 8 won by his Republican opponent, Alfred M. Landon. FDR won every state except Maine and Vermont. One newspaper editor claimed that Roosevelt " . . . has been all but crowned by the people."

Adding to FDR's personal victory was the huge success of the Democratic Party in the congressional elections. Democrats now outnumbered Republicans four to one. There were so many Democrats in Congress that some had to sit on the Republican side of the aisle.

Taking On the Court

In light of the huge election victories, FDR decided it was time to take on the Supreme Court. He wanted the judicial branch of the federal government to be as cooperative toward his goals as the legislative branch had been in his first term. As early as his second inauguration, FDR confessed that while Chief Justice Hughes was swearing him in, emphasizing the words "promise to support the Constitution of the United States," he wanted to shout, "Yes, but it's the Constitution as *I* understand it, flexible enough to meet any new problem of democracy—not the kind of Constitution your Court has raised up as a barrier to progress and democracy."

FDR had formed a plan to mold the Court into something more to his liking. At first, he kept the plan secret, even from many of his top aides. Finally, on February 4, 1937, FDR called a meeting of congressional leaders and cabinet members. He read to them parts of the message that he was sending to Congress within the hour that proposed major changes in the Supreme Court. Overall, FDR wanted sweeping judicial reforms. In light of to the overwhelming number of cases faced by federal courts, FDR proposed that all federal judges retire by the age of seventy. For every judge who did not retire, the president would appoint another judge to serve alongside the original one.

FDR addressing the Washington masses upon his second inauguration. In his speech, he encouraged the American people to continue "along the road over which they have chosen to advance."

In effect, FDR would then be able to appoint six more Supreme Court justices immediately because six of the current justices were seventy or older. Because many of the decisions against the New Deal were decided by a 5 to 4 majority, adding six more pro–New Deal justices would all but ensure that FDR's programs would be upheld by the Court.

Failed Enterprise

FDR stubbornly held his position on judicial reform. Some of his aides suggested other, less drastic changes, such as a constitutional amendment that allowed Supreme Court rulings to be overridden by a two-thirds vote of Congress, but FDR would not budge. FDR's confidence in his proposals did not translate to public support. From the beginning, critics such as former president Herbert Hoover and other Republicans charged that FDR was merely trying to pack the court with cronies, or old friends and political allies. Even Democrats expressed their misgivings. Said Democratic Representative Samuel B. Pettengill of Indiana of FDR's plan: "A packed jury, a packed court, and a stuffed ballot box are all on the same moral plane. This is more power than a good man should want or a bad man should have."

FDR tried to rally the people to his cause. He gave a Fireside Chat on March 9 to talk about his judicial reforms. He said: "Our difficulty with the Court today rises not from the Court as an institution but from human beings within it. . . . This plan of mine is no attack on the Court; it seeks to restore the Court to its rightful and historic place in our Constitutional Government.'" Unfortunately for FDR, his appeal had no effect on the proposal's popularity.

"This is more power than a good man should want or a bad man should have."

By July, the whole scheme was scrapped. This was a major disappointment in FDR's administration—his political instincts, usually so accurate, had failed him completely. In a twist of fate, however, before long the justices began to retire on their own. FDR was thus able to appoint his own choices to the Court after all.

Foreign Worries

Right after the court-packing fiasco, FDR tried to make the best of the situation and to move forward resolutely. In October, he changed the subject on a national level, calling people's attention to the events taking place in Europe and Asia.

Back in 1933, around the same time that FDR had become president of the United States, Adolf Hitler had become **chancellor** of Germany. Just as FDR promised Americans a New Deal, Hitler promised Germans that he would build a German empire, the **Nazi Third Reich**. Germans were still bitter about the terms of their defeat in World War I. The stock market crash in the United States had also created economic problems for Germany. When the United States began collecting on the loans it had made to Germany, the German economy collapsed. The lack of jobs, financial hardships, and old resentments made the German people open to Hitler's promises.

Adolf Hitler (left) with senior Nazi officials, Hermann Goering (second from left) and Joseph Goebbels (right). Hitler's invasion of Poland in 1939 plunged Europe into war.

Hitler had quickly made himself the master of the German people. Dissent was silenced by influencing the press, jailing critics, and even murdering opponents. He blamed Germany's defeat in World War I on Jews and Communists, and working against the agreements made at the end of that war, Hitler rebuilt the German army. A conflict seemed unavoidable, but no one fully understood when it would happen or on what scale.

CHAPTER 10

War Clouds Gathering

I have seen war on land and sea. I have seen blood running from the wounded. . . . I hate war. . . .

Just as Hitler's **dictatorship** was gaining power in Germany and parts of Europe, similar things were happening in Italy and Japan. Italy's dictator, Benito Mussolini, established total control of his country's government, and in 1935, he invaded the African kingdom of Ethiopia. On the other side of the globe, Japan's emperor, Hirohito, invaded and took control of nearby Korea and Manchuria.

For many years, Americans paid little attention to the problems in other parts of the world. They were still trying to pull themselves up from the lingering effects of the Great Depression. Though the New Deal programs were helping the situation, the Depression still was not over.

There was a general feeling that the dictatorships in Germany, Italy, and Japan could not impact the United States. After all, two oceans insulated the country, and most Americans felt that

Italian fascist leader Benito Mussolini began his political life as a pacifist, but changed his views after the outbreak of World War I.

the foreign threats were too distant to be dangerous. Americans bitterly remembered World War I and wanted to avoid another war at all costs.

For the most part, FDR agreed that war should be avoided. During the 1936 campaign, he said, "I have seen war on land and sea. I have seen blood running from the wounded. . . . I hate war. . . . I have passed unnumbered hours, I shall pass unnumbered hours, thinking and planning how war may be kept from this Nation." Still, by 1938, FDR realized the dangers posed by the foreign threats. Two years earlier, he had written his ambassador in Berlin, "Everything seems to have broken loose again in your part of the world. All the experts say there will be no war, but as president, I have to be ready, just like a fire department."

" All the experts say there will be no war, but as president, I have to be ready, just like a fire department."

FDR knew it would not be enough to assume that war could not come to the United States—action would be required sooner or later. In the fall of 1938, Roosevelt told the American public that geographic and political distance, or isolation, from the events of Europe and Asia was not enough to protect them. He also said that **neutrality**, or not taking sides, was like ignoring that these dictatorships were taking over peaceful countries around the world. Americans, however, did not see the situation similarly. The *Wall Street Journal* wrote to recommend that FDR "stop foreign meddling." The Veterans of Foreign Wars began a petition to the government with the motto, "Keep America Out of War." Their goal was to collect 25 million signatures on their formal request to the government to stay out of the war.

A Sad Man

In mid-1940, FDR met with the leaders of the American Youth Congress, who opposed American involvement in the war in Europe. One young man charged that if the president was spending billions on guns and ships then he would be forgetting to help the American people. FDR answered by comparing himself to Abraham Lincoln: "I think the impression was that Lincoln was a pretty sad man because he could not do all he wanted to do at one time, and I think you will find examples where Lincoln had to compromise to gain a little something. . . . He was a politician who was practical enough to get a great many things for this country. He was a sad man because he couldn't get it all at once. And nobody can. . . . Maybe you would make a much better President than I have. Maybe you will, some day. If you ever sit here, you will learn that you cannot, just by shouting from the housetops, get what you want all the time."

FDR offered Lincoln as an example of the difficulties American presidents experience in trying to accomplish as much as they can for the benefit of as many as they can.

Italian fascist leader Benito Mussolini's alliance with Hitler—the two are seen here in Nazi-occupied Yugoslavia—led Italy into World War II, for which it was disastrously ill prepared.

Deterioration Abroad

While Americans argued among themselves, Hitler's armies ran rampant over more and more territory. In 1938, Hitler seized Austria. Later that same year, Hitler, the **führer** and chancellor of Germany; Neville Chamberlain, the British prime minister; Edouard Daladier, the French **premier**; and Mussolini, the Italian dictator, met at the Munich Conference. As a result, Great Britain and France agreed to let Germany control Sudetenland (part of western Czechoslovakia). But within six months of the conference, in March 1939, Hitler had occupied all of Czechoslovakia. At the same time, the civil war that had been raging in Spain ended with the Fascist side—which had been supported by Hitler and Mussolini—winning.

In Germany, Hitler had been persecuting Jews—punishing them for imagined crimes by taking away their rights. Concentration camps were set up to imprison Jews and other people the Nazis considered undesirable. On November 9, 1938, a night known as *Kristallnacht* ("the night of the broken glass"), Nazi storm troopers burned and looted synagogues, Jewish shops, and Jewish offices. The streets were littered with broken glass, giving the night its name. Nearly 100 Jews were murdered and more than 30,000 were arrested and sent to concentration camps. Upon hearing of the violence, FDR said, "The news of the past few days from Germany has deeply shocked public opinion in the United States. . . . I myself could scarcely believe that such things could occur in twentieth century civilization."

Nazi troops march through Warsaw, Poland in October 1939. Warsaw residents were ordered to stay at home during the event, as the Nazis feared an assassination attempt on Hitler.

FDR made efforts to help refugees leave Germany. He organized an international conference with delegates from thirty-two countries to discuss the situation. Unfortunately, apart from Denmark and Holland, no country was willing to relax its immigration laws to welcome refugees. Even in the United States, Congress would not allow immigration quotas to change to accommodate refugees. In general, Americans felt that, with the Depression lingering, there were already too many mouths to feed and not enough jobs to go around.

Working Behind the Scenes

FDR understood the American position. Rather than fighting public opinion, he tried to do what he could within the existing system. He forced the State Department, which deals with foreign affairs and immigration issues, to bend immigration rules to allow thousands of refugees fleeing the Nazis to enter the United States. Unfortunately, thousands more refugees were refused entry.

On September 1, 1939, Hitler invaded Poland. Two days later, Great Britain and France declared war on Germany. Eight other countries had joined them in less than a week, and together the countries became known as the Allied Powers, or the Allies. World War II had now officially begun. FDR, as well as the vast majority of Americans, hoped for a victory by the Allied Powers over Germany and Italy, which had just united. However, no one really knew what would come next.

"There is a general feeling of sitting quiet and waiting to see what the morrow will bring forth."

As president, FDR was limited in what he could do to support the Allies. After Italy had invaded Ethiopia, Americans were so keen on staying out of the conflict that Congress passed the Neutrality Act of 1935. This act banned American citizens from selling arms to countries involved in an international war. In 1939, this meant that the United States could not sell weapons to Great Britain or France—even though it was almost certain that the Allies could not continue the war with Germany without American weapons. Said FDR: "I regret that Congress passed the Neutrality Act. I regret equally that I signed it."

To deal with the situation, FDR called a special session of Congress in 1939, after Germany had taken over Poland. He had been lining up support and finally was able to get the ban on weapons sales in the Neutrality Act repealed, or abolished. The only condition was that countries who bought American weapons had to pay in cash and carry the arms away on their own ships. This "cash-and-carry" policy went into effect that November. Still, it was not clear how involved in the war the United States would get. FDR wrote that fall: "Here in Washington the White House is very quiet. There is a general feeling of sitting quiet and waiting to see what the morrow will bring forth."

That year, FDR also received a letter from the famous scientist, Albert Einstein. Einstein proposed that a new weapon, more powerful than anything the world had ever seen, be developed for the war effort. FDR ordered that the weapon be built but kept the project top secret.

Physicist Albert Einstein, whose letter to Roosevelt instigated the Manhattan Project.

The Manhattan Project

Following Einstein's suggestions, the weapon FDR ordered built was an atomic bomb, or A-bomb. The Manhattan Engineering District, or as it became better known, the Manhattan Project, was the name of the government research project that developed the first atomic bomb for the United States.

Some of the scientists working on the Manhattan Project included Albert Einstein, J. Robert Oppenheimer, Enrico Fermi, Leo Szilard, Edward Teller, and Eugene Wigner, all brilliant scientists in their fields. Interestingly, Einstein was Jewish and had fled Nazi Germany; Fermi had emigrated from Italy after **anti-Semitic** laws were passed that threatened Fermi's Jewish wife; and Szilard, Teller, and Wigner were Jewish refugees from Hungary. Had they not been driven from their homes by Nazi persecution, many of the Manhattan Project scientists would not have been in the United States.

The Manhattan Project designed, produced, and detonated three atomic bombs. The first, called "Trinity," was used in the first nuclear test near Alamogordo, New Mexico. The second and third, "Little Boy" and "Fat Man," were the bombs detonated over the Japanese cities of Hiroshima and Nagasaki.

Upon hearing of the destruction caused by the bombs, Einstein—whose letter to FDR started the whole project— lamented, "I could burn my fingers that I wrote that first letter to Roosevelt."

Albert Einstein with the director of the Manhattan Project, J. Robert Oppenheimer. Einstein later attempted to warn FDR about the consequences of dropping an atomic bomb.

Another Election Year

In January 1940, it was time for another State of the Union address. In it, FDR warned that neutrality could not be absolute. He explained " . . . there is a vast difference between keeping out of war and pretending that this war is none of our business. . . . I ask that all of us everywhere think things through with the single aim of how best to serve the future of our own nation. . . . For it becomes clearer and clearer that the future world will be a shabby and dangerous place to live in—yes, even for Americans to live in—if it is ruled by force in the hands of a few."

"For it becomes clearer and clearer that the future world will be a shabby and dangerous place to live in— yes, even for Americans to live in—if it is ruled by force in the hands of a few."

As FDR predicted, the world became more dangerous. By spring, Hitler had invaded and occupied Denmark, Norway, Holland, and Belgium. On June 10, German forces were joined by Italian troops to attack France. It took only twelve days to force France to surrender. There seemed to be no stopping Adolf Hitler.

In the United States, Congress approved a **draft**—the Selective Service Act of 1940. This was the first ever peacetime draft, and the act was the first step in preparing the country to join the war. As the country made this major decision regarding the future, FDR made one as well: He decided to run for a third term in office.

CHAPTER 11

A World War Rages

It is for peace I have labored; and it is for peace that I shall labor all the days of my life.

In the midst of the worldwide turmoil, FDR's decision to seek a third term as president came as a surprise to many. After all, no president had ever sought re-election more than once. Eleanor later wrote of FDR's decision process: "I think there was a great see-saw, on the one end, the weariness and the desire to be home, on the other the overwhelming desire to have a hand in the affairs of the world."

FDR explained his intentions at the Democratic National Convention on July 19, 1940: "Lying awake, . . . I have asked myself whether I have the right, as commander in chief of the Army and Navy, to call on men and women to serve their country . . . and, at the same time, decline to serve my country in my own personal capacity, if I am called upon to do so by the people of my country. . . . I have had to admit to myself, and now to state to you, that my conscience will not let me turn my back upon a call to service."

The Republicans nominated a businessman and lawyer from Indiana named Wendell L. Willkie. Willkie was a self-made man who had opposed FDR's New Deal for years. He would be the toughest opponent FDR ever faced in an election.

Battle of Britain

While conventions gathered and nominees were selected in the United States, the war raged on overseas. In mid-June, British Prime Minister Winston Churchill said to the British House of Commons: "[T]he Battle of France is over. I expect the Battle of Britain is about to begin. Upon this battle depends the survival of Christian civilization. . . . If we can stand up to him [Hitler], all Europe may be free and the life of the world may move forward into broad, sunlit uplands. But if we fail, then the whole world, including the United States, and all that we have known and cared for, will sink into the abyss [bottomless pit] of a new Dark Age."

As Churchill predicted, by August, the German Air Force, the *Luftwaffe*, was bombing British airfields, factories, and ports. Later that month, the *Luftwaffe* shifted its focus toward bombing London.

The air raids were destroying Great Britain's warships, leaving the seas undefended and open to Hitler's navy. Churchill turned to FDR for help. Britain needed ships immediately, and the United States was the only nation that could provide them. Without those ships, Great Britain would surely fall to Germany. Said Churchill, "Mr. President, with great respect I must tell you that in the long history of the world this is a thing to do *now*."

British Prime Minister Winston Churchill and FDR sometimes disagreed about what course of action to follow, but that did not interfere with what would become a warm friendship between the two men.

FDR was in a tricky position. Facing re-election, he knew that sending ships to Great Britain might cost him enough votes to lose the presidency. In addition, Congress was firmly against directly aiding the Allies in any way. Still, FDR came up with a plan. On September 3, by executive order and therefore not subject to approval by Congress, he arranged to send fifty old but still functioning World War I **destroyers** to Great Britain. In return, Britain leased a number of naval bases in Bermuda, Newfoundland, the Bahamas, Jamaica, Antigua, St. Lucia, Trinidad, and British Guiana to the United States. Because the arrangement involved a trade rather than an outright sale, FDR was within the letter of the law, if not the spirit. FDR confided to his secretary, Grace Tully, "Congress is going to raise hell about this but even another day's delay may mean the end of civilization."

Victories on Two Fronts

Many people, including Willkie, criticized FDR's actions. They reasoned that sending destroyers to Great Britain marked the end of American neutrality in the war and that the action came without the proper legal steps. One newspaper stated that Roosevelt had committed an act of war and had become America's first dictator.

On the other side of the Atlantic, however, the move was critical. Right after the destroyers were sent, Germany reconsidered its invasion of Great Britain. The final order for the invasion never came. It is unclear whether fifty old ships would have made much of a military difference on their own, but all of a sudden, Hitler was forced to acknowledge that the United States would not sit by as he swallowed Western Europe.

The worst night of the German Blitz (short for *blitzkrieg,* meaning "lightning war") was May 10, 1941, when 3,000 Londoners were killed. Here, a family of survivors surveys the damage that surrounds them.

In the United States, the presidential election was approaching. In September, FDR had enjoyed a comfortable lead over Willkie in public opinion polls. By October, however, Willkie was closing the gap. Starting on October 23, FDR began actively campaigning.

Franklin gave five long speeches in which he recounted his accomplishments as president, criticized his opponent for accusing him of being too eager to join the Allies in war, and called for national unity. Finally, he reinforced his support of neutrality by saying that he was following the platform of the Democratic Party: "We will not participate in foreign wars . . . except in case of attack." He repeated that he had always labored for peace and would continue to do so for the rest of his life.

On Election Day, fifty million voters—more than ever before—arrived at the polls. Once again, they threw their support behind FDR. He won the election by 5 million popular votes and won 449 electoral votes.

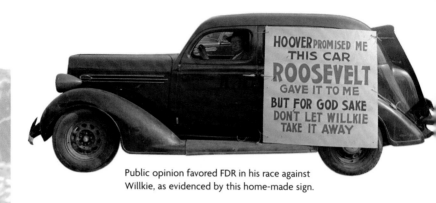

Public opinion favored FDR in his race against Willkie, as evidenced by this home-made sign.

Helping Out

After the election, FDR was determined to aid the Allies as much as possible. In his 1941 State of the Union address, he outlined the "Four Freedoms" he envisioned for the world in the future: freedom of speech and expression everywhere; freedom of religion for everyone everywhere; freedom from want; and freedom from fear. FDR also stated that he believed in " a world-wide reduction of armaments [weapons] to such a point and in such a thorough fashion that no nation will be in a position to commit an act of physical aggression against any neighbor. . . . "

By December 1940, Great Britain was almost bankrupt. The earlier American cash-and-carry policy would not be useful anymore. FDR came up with a solution to the problem—the United States would lend or lease guns and ships to Great Britain until the end of the war. To explain the reasoning for this move, FDR said, "Suppose my neighbor's home catches fire, and I have a length of garden hose four or five hundred feet away. If he can take my garden hose and connect it up with his hydrant, I may help him put out his fire. Now, what do I do? I don't say to him before that operation, 'Neighbor, my garden hose cost me fifteen dollars, you have to pay me fifteen dollars for it.' I don't want fifteen dollars—I want my garden hose back after the fire is over. . . . If it goes through the fire all right . . . he gives it back to me and thanks me. . . . But suppose it gets smashed up during the fire? . . . He says, 'All right, I will replace it.' "

FDR pushed Congress to pass the Lend-Lease Act in March 1941. Military aid to Great Britain increased at once. Still, that year was a hard one for the Allies. Germany had overrun Yugoslavia and Greece in April, and in June, German forces were driving deep into Russia. Nazi submarines, called U-boats, sank 756 Allied ships in the first half of the year.

Though most Americans still wanted to stay out of the war, the United States was slipping into an undeclared war in the Atlantic. In September 1941, FDR ordered American destroyers that were escorting supply **convoys** from the United States to Britain to shoot Nazi U-boats on sight. In October, two American destroyers were attacked by U-boats; one of them, the *Reuben James,* sank after being torpedoed. These hostilities moved the United States closer to war with Germany.

Personal Loss

On September 6, 1941, Franklin took a small break from his worries over the state of the world to visit his mother, Sara, at Springwood. She had been ailing, and Eleanor had summoned Franklin to be with her.

The *Bismarck,* the most famous German battleship of WWII, inflicted much damage on British ships until she was finally sunk in May 1941.

Franklin with his mother, Sara, in 1933. The busy president was nonetheless able to be with his mother when she died.

Franklin chatted happily with Sara all morning and part of the afternoon. By 9:30 that night, however, Sara had developed a blood clot in her lung. She died on September 7, with Franklin by her side. Minutes after her death, the largest oak tree on the Roosevelt property toppled to the ground.

Franklin did not break down at the funeral. A few days later, he was brought a box with his mother's handwriting on it. Inside there were locks of Franklin's hair clipped in childhood, beloved toys, and his christening gown. Franklin's eyes filled with tears. It was the first time anyone on his staff remembered seeing him cry. For more than a year afterward, Franklin wore a black armband to show his sorrow and respect for his mother.

Hit at Home

On September 27, 1940, Germany, Italy, and Japan entered into the Tripartite Pact, or three-party agreement. Up to this point the three countries had been acting and fighting as independent powers. Now newly united, they had joined to form the Axis Powers in a unified force against the Allies. Japan began to attack all across the Far East, while Germany and Italy continued their wars in Europe and Africa. By 1941, Japan had occupied French Indochina (present-day Vietnam, Cambodia, and Laos) and posed a threat to the American-controlled Philippines as well as to British and Dutch territories nearby.

FDR tried to negotiate peace with Japan to prevent further aggression against America. In the meantime, American cryptographers, or code breakers, had broken Japanese codes and were intercepting and reading Japanese military dispatches. There were hints in the messages that the Japanese were planning some kind of large military action in the Pacific.

Enigma

During World War II, the armies of both the Allies and the Axis Powers used codes to send their messages, in order to prevent them from being read by the enemy in case they were intercepted. Cryptographers were responsible for breaking those codes to retrieve the information.

The German army used codes that were particluarly difficult to break. These codes were generated by machines called *rotor ciphers*, which look like typewriters but had several disks inside that rotated to create codes. The codes were so complex that they could not be decoded without the use of another rotor cipher. Further, the settings on both the rotor cipher used to generate the code and the one used to decipher the code had to be identical, or the code could not be broken.

The German rotor ciphers were commonly called *Enigma machines*. The codes generated by Enigma machines were first broken by Polish cryptographers in 1932. Later, Poland shared information on the Enigma machines with France and Britain, which helped the Allies continue to break German codes.

Code Talkers

During World War II, the United States Marine Corps developed a code based on the language of the Navajo, a Native American group. It was a fairly simply code, in that Navajo words were used in place of English letters. These letters, in turn, spelled out the coded messages. Several Navajo words were used to represent each letter, and other words represented common military terms. The Native Americans who served in the military to transmit and decipher the codes were called *code talkers*.

The code created from the Navajo language was used in operations in the Pacific, especially against the Japanese. The code proved to be unbreakable by Japanese cryptographers because they had no knowledge of the Navajo language. There were no native speakers of the Navajo language outside the United States, and the Japanese had never encountered anything similar. Because every letter had several possible corresponding Navajo words, it was even more difficult for cryptographers to decode the messages. Said former code talker Samuel Billison, "They came up with a code nobody broke. Not the Japanese, not the Marines, not the Navy, not even other Navajo. You had to study the code to know what was being sent."

No one, however, anticipated what kind of action Japan would take. It was a total surprise at dawn on December 7, 1941, when 350 Japanese bombers and airplanes approached the American naval base at Pearl Harbor, Hawaii. The ensuing battle was hopeless for the Americans. Caught unaware, nearly all of the American Pacific Fleet—19 warships and 188 planes—were destroyed or damaged in the attack. Most of the planes were destroyed while still on the ground, and the ships were still tied to docks or moored in the bay. In addition, more than 3,500 Americans were killed or wounded.

By the next morning, it became clear that Pearl Harbor was not an isolated attack. Japanese forces launched attacks against Malaya, Hong Kong, Guam, the Philippine Islands, Wake Island, and Midway Island. It seemed that the entire Pacific was under siege.

FDR was personally shaken by the attack on Pearl Harbor. When advisers told him that the whole navy had been destroyed, FDR put his head in his hands at his desk and said, "My God, my God, how did it happen? . . . Now I'll go down in history disgraced." Informing his cabinet proved very difficult for FDR. Labor Secretary Frances Perkins remembered that Roosevelt appeared to be having difficulty in getting out the words that put him on record as knowing the navy was caught unawares.

Japanese Type 99 carrier bomber, in action during the raid on Pearl Harbor.

Part of the destruction wrought by the surprise attack on Pearl Harbor, Hawaii, on December 7, 1941, a "date that will live in infamy."

On December 8, FDR solemnly appeared before a joint session of Congress. In a black notebook, he held the text of the speech he had worked on until the last possible moment. When he stood at the podium, he gripped it so tightly his knuckles turned white. With a grave expression he faced the silent chamber and began his speech: "Yesterday, December 7, 1941—a date which will live in infamy—the United States of America was suddenly and deliberately attacked by naval and air forces of the Empire of Japan. . . . As Commander in Chief of the Army and Navy I have directed that all measures be taken for our defense. . . . No matter how long it may take us to overcome this premeditated invasion, the American people in their righteous might will win through to absolute victory. . . . I ask that the Congress declare that since the unprovoked and dastardly attack by Japan on Sunday, December 7, 1941, a state of war has existed between the United States and the Japanese Empire."

FDR signing the declaration of war against Japan, which Congress approved only thirty-three minutes after the president spoke to them.

Congress took just thirty-three minutes to agree to FDR's request. The United States was now at war with Japan. On the same day, Great Britain declared war on Japan; and three days later, Germany and Italy declared war on the United States.

CHAPTER 12

The Commander in Chief

The only limit to our realization of tomorrow will be our doubts of today. Let us move forward with strong and active faith.

Even after the United States entered the war, things did not go well for the Allies. They suffered setbacks in the Pacific as Japan took control of the Philippines, Malaya, Burma, and the Dutch East Indies (now Indonesia) and occupied the American islands of Guam and Wake. Nazi U-boats continued to wreak havoc in the Atlantic, even striking ships within sight of Manhattan. Nazi tanks rumbled toward Moscow and Leningrad.

Everywhere, Americans were faced with uncertainty. Newspaper headlines from *The New York Times* included everything from "42,000,000 Are Seen Ready for War Job; Gallup Poll Finds Veritable Niagara of Human Power Eager to Work Free" to "Nazi Sees Victory; Hitler Warns U.S. of U-boat Drive." People did not know whether to be confident or cautious about the war prospects.

On a personal note, for the Roosevelts the war meant not only risking the lives of millions of Americans, but risking the lives of their sons. All four of FDR's sons—James, Elliott, Franklin Jr., and John—served in the military in World War II. All four saw active duty and were recognized for bravery. Eleanor in particular was worried that her sons would not all come back, because the probability was that they would not.

Preparing for War

In the United States, FDR used the same determination to prepare the country for war that he had shown in pushing through New Deal proposals, and the American people were just as eager to follow their president in war preparations as they had been to make the New Deal work. Ten days after Pearl Harbor, FDR

All four of Franklin's sons served in World War II—and returned home safely. Shown clockwise from top left: Elliot; James; John; and Franklin, Jr.

Doing Our Part at Home

When FDR sent the U.S. military to war, he knew that civilians would have to make sacrifices to support the war effort. He asked Americans to do without, or **ration**, a variety of things. Food items such as meat, butter, cheese, and coffee were rationed. To conserve food and grow more, Americans were encouraged to plant "victory gardens" in backyards, vacant lots, and public parks to grow vegetables and fruits. These victory gardens produced more than 1 billion tons of food.

Americans were encouraged to contribute to the war effort in every possible way. Here, a woman donates stockings so the military can make gunpowder bags.

At salvage drives, Americans collected tin cans, old cars, bed frames, radiators, pots, pipes, and tin-foil from gum wrappers. These items were melted down to help supply the military's need for steel and aluminum for everything from tanks to canteens. Women went without nylon stockings so that the material could be used for parachutes or gunpowder bags. The speed limit in most of the United States was lowered to 35 miles per hour so gasoline could be saved to run military jeeps and other vehicles.

Finally, Americans accepted income tax increases to help pay for the war. It was during World War II that the withholding system of payroll deductions—in which the government keeps a certain amount of money from each paycheck to cover a person's yearly income tax—was put into place. Even though Americans now had less money in their paychecks, they also supported the war by buying war bonds. Approximately one out of every two people—85 million in all—bought at least one war bond during World War II. These purchases produced $185.7 billion for the government. In addition, civilians produced actual goods for the military effort: 2,832,000 trucks, 15 million guns, 41 billion bullets, 224,000 artillery pieces, 324,000 aircraft, and 88,000 tanks.

summoned coal miners, shipbuilders, airplane engine workers, and others, along with their employers, to the White House. The workers had been on strike since before the attack, but FDR told both sides that it would be a "thrilling thing" if they could sort through their differences and unite to produce what the country needed to fight this war.

In fact, preparations for war went on all across the nation. The country's factories and shipyards were turned into production centers for airplanes, weapons, warships, and tanks. War production in the United States supplied all the Allies with the resources to continue fighting.

The United States also mobilized a massive military force— more than 15 million people at its peak. Between the jobs in war production and those in the military, unemployment virtually vanished. There were so many jobs to do that large numbers of women were forced into factory work— jobs that were held only by men before the war. The transition for women from homemakers and clerical workers into these traditionally male industries was difficult for everyone, but the demand was so great that American women were desperately needed to keep the factories running and to help make airplanes, tanks, jeeps, and

Gladys Theus was known for her welding speed and efficiency at the Kaiser Company Permanente Metals Corporation in Oakland, California. The war created many new opportunities for minority workers.

During the war, women had previously unheard-of employment opportunities, such as the woman here shown working on attack bombers at the Douglas Aircraft plant in Long Beach, California.

other necessities for the war effort. By 1945, women made up 36 percent of the country's total workforce.

Minority workers also benefited from the war's needs, especially African Americans. On June 25, 1941, FDR signed an executive order to create the Fair Employment Practices Committee (FEPC). This order declared that "there shall be no discrimination in the employment of workers in defense industries or government because of race, creed, color, or national origin." This order effectively outlawed racial discrimination in any defense industry receiving federal contracts and marked the first time that the federal government made an effort to enforce civil rights.

America's Camps

While the war was helpful to some minority groups because it created new jobs for them, it also created huge problems for others—namely, Japanese Americans and Japanese resident aliens. After Pearl Harbor, the country's population directed a great deal of anger toward Japanese Americans. Even though there was no proof that they had any involvement in the attack, their ancestry was enough to convict them in the minds of many Americans.

In early 1942, to prevent any Japanese "spies" from helping the enemy, it was decided that all Japanese Americans should be moved to special camps and detained there. Eleanor Roosevelt

During the war, many Japanese Americans and Japanese resident aliens were sent to internment camps This action is now regarded as one of the darker chapters in U.S. history.

strongly opposed this decision and told her husband of her misgivings. FDR, however, was in a difficult position. The public supported this move, and much of FDR's power as president came from the strong public support he enjoyed. FDR felt he had no choice but to order the forced relocation to policed camps of 120,000 people, half of them American citizens, without charge or trial.

Eleanor continued to disapprove of the internment of Japanese Americans. Though hers was a very unpopular position, she persisted in her criticisms of the government's actions. In 1943, she wrote, "I can well understand the bitterness of people who have lost loved ones at the hands of the Japanese military authorities. . . . It is not hard to understand why people living here in hourly anxiety for those they love have difficulty in viewing our Japanese problem objectively, but for the honor of our country, the rest of us must do so. . . . Japanese-Americans may be no more Japanese than a German-American is German, or an Italian-American is Italian. . . . We have no common race in this country, but we have an ideal to which all of us are loyal. . . . We cannot progress if we look down upon any group of people among us because of race or religion."

Helping the Victims

FDR's primary objective was to win the war, which often meant sacrificing his personal ideals. Though FDR remained very concerned about the victims of the Nazis as the war continued, he could not do much to directly aid them.

Reports were coming in from Europe about Nazi death camps where tens of thousands of Jews and other people considered undesirable by the Nazis were imprisoned, tortured, and murdered. The State Department, however, discredited these reports. It was beyond most people's imaginations to believe that murders on this scale could occur. Even when FDR heard in 1942 about Hitler's "Final Solution" to exterminate all Jewish people, he could not believe it at first. More details continued to trickle in, however, and soon, the truth could not be denied.

In 1944, the Treasury Department secretary, Henry Morgenthau, came to FDR with a report about Jewish people trying to flee Nazi-controlled territories. The report said that the State Department had not only failed to use government

Jewish prisoners at the Buchenwald concentration camp. Elie Weisel, later a world-renowned author and humanitarian, can be seen circled on the second row from the bottom.

Children who would survive the infamous Auschwitz concentration camp, wearing prison jackets that previously belonged to adult prisoners.

resources to rescue Jews from Hitler, but it had also gone so far as to prevent their rescue from him.

FDR immediately took action, though he was still limited in what actions he could take. Within six days, he gave an executive order to create the War Refugee Board, which would be responsible for rescuing victims of the Nazis. Overall, the War Refugee Board saved the lives of more than 200,000 Jewish people and 20,000 non-Jews.

The Turning Tide

On February 23, 1942, FDR gave another Fireside Chat. Before the address, the White House announced that FDR would be talking about many foreign countries and locations, and that

Americans should have their maps handy. Map and atlas sales soared as more than 60 million people prepared to listen to the president's words.

In his address, FDR once again connected with the public through his conversational style. He explained where in the world the Axis Powers had conquered and where Americans were battling. However, he glossed over the harsh realities in an effort to keep Americans hopeful.

Finally, after so many setbacks, in late 1942, the tide of the war began to turn and the Allies started gaining ground. The Japanese, Germans, and Italians were being driven back on all fronts. By January 1943, it was possible for FDR to travel to Casablanca, in Morocco, to meet with Churchill in person. He became the first president to leave the United States during wartime, the first to fly, and the first since Lincoln to travel to an active war zone. In Casablanca, FDR and Churchill decided that the only way the war would end would be with the unconditional surrender of the Axis Powers.

In November 1943, FDR and Churchill met again in Teheran, Iran. This time, they also met with Joseph Stalin, the leader of Russia, making it the first "Big Three" conference. Various military issues regarding the next phase of the war were discussed, as well as larger political issues about what would happen in peacetime. After the conference, the three leaders issued a joint statement, saying: "As to peace—we are sure that our **concord** will win an enduring peace. We recognize fully the supreme responsibility resting upon us and all the United Nations to make a peace which will command the goodwill of the overwhelming mass of the peoples of the world and banish the scourge and terror of war for many generations. . . . No power on earth can prevent our destroying the German armies by land, their U-boats by sea, and their war plants from the air. Our attack will be relentless and increasing . . . .We came here with hope and determination. We leave here, friends in fact, in spirit and in purpose."

FDR came back from Teheran in an optimistic mood. In a Fireside Chat on December 24, 1943, he told the American people that the United States and its allies represented more than three-quarters of the total population of Earth. As long as those strong nations stayed together in determination to keep world peace, no aggressor nation could arise and start another world war. The strong countries of the world would not dominate the weaker ones.

"We came here with hope and determination. We leave here, friends in fact, in spirit and in purpose."

The U.S. Army's First Infantry Division lands on Omaha Beach on June 6, 1944—D-Day.

One Last Run

By the end of 1943, victory was in sight for the Allies. On September 8, the Italian forces had surrendered, and by October 13, Italy declared war on Germany, its former ally. British bombers were pounding Berlin from the air, and Russians troops were beating German forces back.

On June 6, 1944—D-Day—the long-awaited invasion of western Europe by the Allied Powers began. Under the command of United States General Dwight D. Eisenhower, more than 150,000 troops crossed the English Channel and landed on the beaches of Normandy in France.

General—later President—Dwight D. Eisenhower addressing American paratroopers in England on D-Day.

The area was under German control, and the Allies suffered heavy casualties. It took many grueling weeks of battle, in which success was often measured in yards—not miles—gained, but eventually, the Allies won; and the most powerful German force in France, the Seventh Army, was almost completely destroyed. Paris was liberated on August 25. On the other side of Europe, Russians forces were advancing toward Warsaw, Poland. In the Pacific, Japanese troops were driven out of Saipan and Guam; and the Allies had landed in the Philippines.

While the war inched toward its conclusion, FDR was faced with another presidential election. His health was clearly deteriorating, with dark circles visible under his eyes and a persistent cough and trembling hands apparent. Still, the job at hand—winning the war—was not yet done, and FDR agreed to run again. With Missouri Senator Harry S. Truman as his running mate, FDR said, "If the people command me to continue in this office and in this war I have as little right to withdraw as the soldier has to leave his post in the line."

FDR's opponent was Republican Thomas E. Dewey, governor of New York. Dewey's campaign tried to make an issue of FDR seeking a fourth term in office, but the voters for the most part did not seem to care. FDR won this election as well, by more than 3.6 million popular votes. Shortly after midnight on Election Day, FDR told his supporters in Hyde Park, where he awaited the election results, "It looks like I will have to come back here on a train from Washington for four more years . . . . It will always be worth it."

> "It looks like I will have to come back here on a train from Washington for four more years.It will always be worth it."

FDR (center, seated) outside Lividia Palace with Winston Churchill (left, seated) and Joseph Stalin (right, seated) in a seemingly relaxed moment during the Yalta Conference in 1945.

More Work to Do

After his fourth inauguration, FDR was on the move again. This time, he headed to Yalta, a Russian town on the shores of the Black Sea, to meet with Churchill and Stalin for another Big Three conference.

World War II was almost at an end, at least in Europe. Berlin was being bombed around the clock, reducing the city to a pile of rubble. Hitler's armies had been beaten back on every front, except for a few pockets of resistance in northern Italy and Hungary. On the Asian front, American forces had already liberated Manila in the Philippines and were using bombers to blast Japanese cities.

In Yalta, FDR hoped to gain Russia's cooperation to build a lasting peace. The conference ran for eight days, from February 4 to February 11. During this time, FDR discussed the formation of a new organization called the United Nations with Churchill and Stalin. The United Nations would serve to ensure world peace from then on.

FDR's health, however, was still failing. The stress of the war years, his illness, and the pressures of building peace weighed heavily on him. FDR's frailty was visible to those at the conference, although the president was still able to charm them with his wit.

After returning from the Yalta Conference, FDR addressed Congress. Said historian James MacGregor Burns, "Roosevelt's voice was strangely thick and blurred. . . . He stumbled and halted; he ad-libbed irrelevancies. At times his face and words flamed with the old eloquence; then it seemed to ebb away." FDR sat during the address rather than standing, and for the first time ever, he even acknowledged his disability: "I hope that you will pardon me for an unusual posture of sitting down during the presentation of what I want to say. I know that you will realize that it makes it a lot easier for me in not having to carry about ten pounds of steel around on the bottom of my legs, and also because of the fact that I have just completed a fourteen thousand-mile trip." FDR was clearly ailing, and soon afterward, he decided to go to a resort in Warm Springs, Georgia, for a much-needed rest.

Final Days

On April 12, 1945, at Warm Springs, artist Elizabeth Shoumatoff was painting a portrait of FDR as he worked on a speech. He wrote about his hopes for his country in the aftermath of World War II: "Today, as we move against the terrible scourge

FDR's horse-drawn casket during his Pennsylvania Avenue funeral procession.

of war—as we go forward toward the greatest contribution that any generation of human beings can make in this world—the contribution of lasting peace, I ask you to keep up your faith. . . . Let us move forward with strong and active faith."

FDR did not live long enough to give that speech. At 12:45 p.m., FDR announced that he would pose for another fifteen minutes. Before the time was up, he complained of a headache and he said, "I have a terrific pain in the back of my head." He then slumped forward in his chair and never regained consciousness. Franklin Delano Roosevelt died from a massive cerebral hemorrhage.

The official notice of his death listed FDR as a war casualty: "Army-Navy Dead: ROOSEVELT, Franklin D., Commander in Chief, wife, Mrs. Anna Eleanor Roosevelt, the White House."

The End of an Era

Eleanor was in Washington at the time of Franklin's death. She wrote to her sons, still away at war, to give them the news: "He did his job to the end, as he would expect you to do." Later that evening, she informed Vice President Harry Truman that FDR was dead and asked if it was appropriate for her to take a government plane down to Warm Springs. Truman assured her it was.

Shortly after Truman was sworn in as president in Washington, D.C., Eleanor left for Warm Springs. She spent ten minutes alone with her husband's body and composed herself with the dignity that would carry her through the grieving process. She chose new clothes for FDR—a double-breasted blue suit, a white shirt, and a blue and white tie.

On the morning of April 13, FDR's body was placed in a flag-draped coffin and loaded onto the presidential train. The coffin could be seen by the thousands of onlookers who lined the train tracks. After a White House funeral on April 14, FDR's body was transported back to Hyde Park by train. Standing guard over him on this last journey were four servicemen from the army, navy, marines, and coast guard. On the morning of April 15, FDR was buried in his mother's rose garden at his childhood home.

FDR did not live to see the end of World War II. A little more than two weeks after his burial, Russian soldiers were closing in on Hitler's bunker in Berlin, and the German dictator shot himself to avoid capture. Germany signed an unconditional surrender to the Allies on May 7, 1945.

FDR's death spared him from having to give the order to use the powerful secret weapon—the atomic bomb. That duty fell to Harry Truman, now President Truman. Many factors influenced Truman's decision, including the advice of political and military leaders, an American public that was eager for an end to the war, and the possibility of a quick victory over Japan. Atomic bombs were dropped on Hiroshima on August 6 and on Nagasaki on August 9. The impact of the bombs was devastating; more than 130,000 people were killed at Hiroshima and approximately

President Truman gave the order to use the newly developed atomic bombs against Japan, a decision that still has repercussions today. Shown here is the explosion over Nagasaki in 1945.

another 80,000 died at Nagasaki. Five days later, Japan surrendered unconditionally. World War II was over.

"I felt as if he knew me..."

The world had moved on without FDR, but it was clear that he would never be forgotten. He had been president for so long that for many Americans, he was the only president they could remember. Because FDR had spent so much time courting public opinion by speaking directly to the people, Americans mourned him more as a personal friend than they had any previous leader. On the night of Roosevelt's death, a young soldier stood before the White House with his eyes full of tears for the death of a man he had never met. He said, "I felt as if I knew him. I felt as if he knew me—and I felt as if he liked me."

FDR had led the United States through two of the most

important events of the twentieth century: the Great Depression and World War II. His leadership made it possible for the United States to emerge from these crises greater than ever. He championed programs that gave opportunities to poor people, protected the common man, and promoted racial and gender equality. His personal handicap never hampered him in his pursuit of what was best for the country.

After FDR's death, an editorial appeared in *The New York Times*, saying, "Men will thank God on their knees a hundred years from now that Franklin D. Roosevelt was in the White House. It was his hand, more than that of any other single man, that built the great coalition of the United Nations. It was his leadership which inspired free men in every part of the world to fight with greater hope and courage. Gone is the fresh and spontaneous interest which this man took, as naturally as he breathed air, in the troubles and the hardships and the disappointments and the hopes of little men and humble people."

The Franklin Delano Roosevelt Memorial in Washington, D.C. Roosevelt is depicted with his much-loved dog, Fala.

Glossary

anti-Semitic—feeling hostility toward Jews as a religious and ethnic group.

chancellor—the chief minister of state in some European countries.

concord—an agreement, usually concerning peaceful relations between countries.

convoys—groups of ships traveling together for self-protection, usually in wartime.

destroyers—small, fast warships used to protect larger ships in convoys, usually armed with five-inch guns, depth charges, and torpedoes.

dictatorship—a form of government in which absolute power is controlled by one person or a small group.

draft—a system for selecting individuals for required military service.

electoral votes—votes from each state that elect the president and vice president of the United States. There are 538 votes in the Electoral College.

führer—means "leader" in German; title used by Adolf Hitler to define his position of absolute authority in Germany's Third Reich.

Great Depression—the worldwide economic crisis that began with the U.S. stock market crash in 1929 and continued through the 1930s.

inaugurated—inducted into office by taking a solemn oath.

labor unions—a group of workers united to gain better wages and working conditions.

Nazi Third Reich—the regime in Germany under Adolf Hitler (1933–1945).

neutrality—the state of refraining from taking sides or building alliances in a war or a dispute.

party bosses—leaders in a political party who control votes and appointments; usually they have a reputation for corruption.

premier—in many countries, the person who is head of state.

ration—to reduce the amount of food, gasoline, and other things each person used each day.

reform—to enact a change to make a government or business work better.

regulations—official rules, laws, or orders created to govern procedures.

stump speeches—political speeches made during a campaign tour.

Bibliography

Alter, Jonathan. *The Defining Moment: FDR's Hundred Days and the Triumph of Hope*. New York: Simon & Schuster, 2006.

Brigham, Daniel T. "Nazi Sees Victory; Hitler Warns U.S. of U-boat Drive."*The New York Times,* Jan 31, 1942.

Black, Conrad. *Franklin Delano Roosevelt: Champion of Freedom*. New York: PublicAffairs, 2003.

_____. "Breaking Soil." *Time*. Nov 26, 1934.

Burns, James MacGregor. *Roosevelt: The Lion and the Fox 1882–1940*. San Diego: Harvest Books, 2002.

Chafe, William H. *Private Lives / Public Consequences*. Cambridge, Massachusetts: Harvard University Press, 2005.

Damon, Allan L. "Presidential Accessibility." *American Heritage*. April 1974. Volume 25, Issue 3.

Day, Donald, ed. *Franklin D. Roosevelt's Own Story*. Boston: Little, Brown and Company, 1951.

Freedman, Russell. *Franklin Delano Roosevelt*. New York: Clarion Books, 1990.

Gallup, George. "42,000,000 Are Seen Ready for War Job; Gallup Poll Finds Veritable Niagara of Human Power Eager to Work Free."*The New York Times* (1857-Current file), Mar 15, 1942.

Goodwin, Doris Kearns. "Person of the Century Runner-Up: Franklin Delano Roosevelt." *Time*. Jan 3, 2000.

Leuchtenburg, William E. *The FDR Years: On Roosevelt and His Legacy*. New York: Columbia University Press, 1997.

Reichers, Maggie. "Eleanor Roosevelt, No Ordinary Woman." *Humanities*. January/Febuary 2000, Volume 21, Number 1.

_____. "Report to the Secretary on the Acquiescence of this Government in the Murder of the Jews (January 13, 1944)." Jewish Virtual Library.

Roosevelt, Eleanor. "A Challenge to American Sportsmanship." *Collier's*. Number 112, October 16, 1943.

Roosevelt, Elliot, ed. *FDR: His Personal Letters, Early Years*. New York: Duell, Sloan and Pearce, 1947.

Ward, Geoffrey C. *Before the Trumpet*. Konecky & Konecky. 1985.

Image Credits

About the Author

Sudipta Bardhan-Quallen completed two biology degrees at the California
Institute of Technology and spent many years enjoying the sunshine of
Southern California. After all that time in Los Angeles, she eventually found
herself at home back east. She now lives in New Jersey with her husband
and children.

She is the author of several books for children. She writes picture books,
science books, biographies, and other nonfiction for children. In her free
time, she enjoys reading, gossiping over hot chocolate, shopping for shoes,
and sleeping in.

INDEX